Famous African Americans
Table of Contents

Correlation to Curriculum

Famous African American	Page	(globe)	(book A)	(flask)	(math)	(palette)	(scroll)	(lightbulb)
Maya Angelou	9	•	•					
Alex Haley	12	•	•					
John Johnson	15	•	•		•		•	•
Toni Morrison	18	•	•					
Gordon Parks	21	•	•				•	
Babyface	25	•	•				•	
Bill Cosby	28	•				•	•	•
Whoopi Goldberg	31	•					•	
Whitney Houston	34	•					•	•
Leontyne Price	37	•		•		•		
Oprah Winfrey	40	•	•					
Tom Bradley	44	•	•			•	•	•
Shirley Chisholm	47	•					•	•
Barbara Jordan	50	•	•				•	
Coretta Scott King	53	•	•				•	
Thurgood Marshall	56	•					•	•
Colin Powell	59	•					•	
Guion Bluford	63	•	•	•				
Mae Jemison	66	•		•			•	
Geraldine Pittman Woods	69	•			•		•	
Dominique Dawes	73	•	•		•		•	
Gail Devers	76	•	•				•	
David Robinson	79	•				•	•	
Emmitt Smith	82	•	•				•	•
Frank Thomas	85	•			•		•	
Tiger Woods	88	•	•				•	

Famous African Americans 5-6, SV 6792-1

About *Famous African Americans*

This book relates historic events in the lives of 26 African Americans. The selections represent African-American achievements in the arts, entertainment, politics, civil rights, the military, science, and sports. The biographical sketches relate not only the achievements of the individuals, but also the drive and effort necessary to accomplish them.

What You Will Find in this Book

• **Learning Assessments** so that you may measure your students' progress for portfolios. There is an overall assessment test, and there are separate assessments at the end of each career grouping.

• **26 biographical events**

• **Activity suggestions** for general study of African Americans and **suggestions for using this book**. There are both independent activities and activities to share.

• **Letters to parents and to students**. The letter to the parents can be copied and sent home with the students. It will create awareness for parents to be open to their children's questions about famous African Americans and to encourage discussion between parents and children. The letter to students is designed to encourage discussion and questions and to stimulate interest about famous African Americans.

Organization

Each biographical event is part of a three-page section that includes the following:

• **the story,**

• **a comprehension exercise,**

• **5 vocabulary words** chosen from each story for further understanding,

• **a research exercise,**

• **and a learning activity** related to the biography.

These activities encompass the curriculum areas of **social studies, language arts, math, science, and art**. The comprehension questions test the students' understanding of what they've read. The research exercises encourage students to think beyond their reading. The activities reinforce the learned materials in fun, challenging, and interesting ways and sometimes introduce new, related materials.

• **Icons** in the **Correlation to Curriculum** and next to each activity will help you find curriculum-related activities.

• **Insets** on each story page either highlight a new fact or give more detail to the story.

• **Answer Key** is on pages 93-96.

Using *Famous African Americans*

Use this book as a tool to show students that people are more alike than different. We all hurt, love, feel fear, experience joy, and desire successes in our lives.

The biographies discuss many careers. Class discussions about different careers can enhance students' understanding of the people and their accomplishments.

You may photocopy each of the lessons for students to secure in a notebook or folder. Some vocabulary has been targeted for further understanding in the comprehension sections, but you may want to introduce some unfamiliar words as well. In each lesson additional research materials are needed to complete an activity. The following activity suggestions provide opportunities to expand the lessons and to get the maximum benefit from this book.

Activity Suggestions

• Encourage students to bring in appropriate newspaper/magazine articles about African Americans in the news. Share them with the class. Hang them on a special bulletin board.

• Have students write a letter to an African American who interests them.

• Invite local African-American achievers to come to the class and tell about their jobs (minister, businessperson, college professor, principal, contractor, etc.).

• Group students for campaign and debate of all angles of an issue that faces your school or town. This assignment may include choosing a leader for each side, campaign signs and slogans, platforms, and a mock election. Some students may have to campaign for an issue on a side with which they disagree. Remind them that there are at least two sides to every issue, that they don't have to change their minds, but that they can develop broad-minded views.

• Post a U.S. map in the room for discussion of where each achiever lived, traveled, and worked.

• Bring in appropriate recordings by Whitney Houston, Leontyne Price, Babyface, Bill Cosby, Toni Morrison, Maya Angelou, and Alex Haley. Find and share samples of poetry or writing from Toni Morrison, Maya Angelou, Alex Haley, Bill Cosby, and Gordon Parks.

• As a follow-up activity for each career-group, have each student find another famous African American in the same field. Allow the students to demonstrate that person's accomplishments in a creative way. The assignment could be completed as writing, artwork (painting, drawing, collage, etc...), photography, musical arrangement, or any other medium of the student's choosing.

• Ask students to select an African-American achiever from their book and create something that represents that person. The student can present the creation to the class and have classmates guess the person's identity.

• Have students talk about how they could become famous Americans. For what would they like to be remembered? How do they plan to achieve their goals? Students should recognize that diligence, hard work, tenacity, integrity, commitment to a goal, and strong will are necessary elements in being successful.

Dear Student:

You're about to have an adventure! You'll be amazed, surprised, and challenged. You're going to see what it takes to make a hero. You'll read about how hard it can be to change history, and then you'll see how rewarding it can be. You'll meet champions, winners, and people who worked quietly to make a big difference. You'll learn about people in science, sports, education, politics, the arts, and the armed forces. You'll learn about famous African Americans. You'll see how these incredible people, sometimes against all odds, made changes that affected and improved the lives of not only African Americans, but of all Americans.

You will take a pre-test to show how much you already know about the famous African Americans discussed in this book. You will also have your knowledge tested as you study the African Americans in each career-group.

Each of the lessons is a one-page story with two pages of activities. The activities give you an opportunity to apply what you have learned and to look at how the accomplishments of others affect you.

Please plan to keep all your lessons in a notebook or folder. You may want to decorate the folder! When you have done all the lessons, you will have the opportunity to show how much you have learned. In order to help you remember the events and the people you will be studying, please talk about them with your family and friends.

Have fun as you begin this adventure. Plan to work hard and to learn everything you can!

Sincerely,

Dear Parents,

To increase your child's understanding of our history and the contributions that African Americans have made, we will be studying 26 famous African Americans. The stories have been written with your child in mind. Each one centers on an important, interesting event. Two activity pages that complete each section will help your child remember his or her reading. They will also encourage your child to think beyond the story and to apply experiences to his/her own life. Your child may be assigned to bring these pages home for completion.

Regardless of whether these lessons are assigned as homework, please ask your child to talk about the stories. Share your own knowledge about famous African Americans. When your child sees that you are interested, it will spark his or her interest even more. If the pages are brought home for completion, please support your child by communicating your expectations that the work be done. You can offer this support by providing a quiet work area and by checking the work when your child has finished.

Since many of the lessons refer to exceptional effort on the part of the individual, you have an opportunity to talk with your child about those qualities which contribute to success in all fields of work. Identification of possible career interests can emerge from these discussions.

Above all, enjoy this time with your child as, together, you learn more about famous African Americans.

Sincerely,

Name _____ Date _____

Test Your Knowledge of Famous African Americans

Write the correct answer to fill in the blanks for questions 1 - 5.

1. Maya Angelou, Alex Haley, Toni Morrison, and Gordon Parks have what in common?

   _____

   _____

2. Bill Cosby and Whoopi Goldberg are pleased when their audiences

   _____ .

3. Shirley Chisholm and Barbara Jordan have made their marks in what profession?

   _____

4. As _____ , Guion Bluford and Mae Jemison have probably seen more of Earth than most people.

5. David Robinson, Emmitt Smith, and Frank Thomas are _____ .

Write a brief answer to questions 6 - 10. Use complete sentences.

6. For what is John Johnson known as a famous African American?

   _____

7. What is the difference between the singing of Whitney Houston and that of

   Leontyne Price? _____

   _____

8. What is one of Colin Powell's greatest achievements? _____

   _____

9. In what area has Geraldine Pittman Woods made her contributions?

   _____

10. When and where might Dominique Dawes and Gail Devers have met?

    _____

Famous African Americans 5-6, SV 6792-1

Name _____ Date _____

Write the name of an African American to correctly complete sentences 11 - 15.

11. The Texas Congresswoman, _____ , was part of the group that held President Nixon responsible for Watergate.

12. The ambition of _____ is to win every golf tournament he plays.

13. _____ wrote *The Learning Tree*.

14. _____ was instrumental in the court's decision that all children could go to the same schools.

15. _____ 's rhythm and blues songs have a soft melody.

Write answers to questions 16-20 on the back of this sheet or on a separate sheet of paper.

16. Name four professions in which African Americans have made contributions in U.S. history.

17. Write three questions that Oprah Winfrey could ask Colin Powell in an interview about his career.

18. Write a brief paragraph about Bill Cosby. Include three or four details about his life.

19. You are a sportscaster. Write four questions that you would ask either Gail Devers, Dominique Dawes, Emmitt Smith, or Frank Thomas during an interview.

20. Many similar characteristics are exhibited by famous African-American role models. Name five.

Maya Angelou
Writer

Maya's hypnotic voice echoed through the Washington, D.C., crowd of 100,000 as she read her poem in perfect rhythmic cadence. She was appealing to the people of the United States—Asians, Africans, Italians, Catholics, Muslims, Jews, Hispanics, Native Americans, rich, poor—everyone. She wanted the people to come together in unity and as a family. The world was watching on television and listening on radio as Maya Angelou read *On the Pulse of Morning*, a poem that she had written for the occasion of the inauguration of the forty-second President of the United States, William "Bill" Jefferson Clinton, January 23, 1993.

Maya Angelou was born Marguerite Johnson in 1928. Her brother, Bailey, who was a year older, called her "My," for "my sister." Soon "My" was lengthened to Maya. When she was three her parents divorced, and she and Bailey were sent to live with their grandmother, Mrs. Annie Henderson, in Stamps, Arkansas. The children called their grandmother Momma. She owned a general store where people gathered to visit and exchange news. Barbers would come and cut men's hair on Saturdays. Maya's life in Stamps was happy and stable.

When Maya was eight, she and Bailey moved to St. Louis, Missouri, to live with their mother. Maya's memories of St. Louis were painful. She was abused by her mother's boyfriend, Mr. Freeman, and had to testify against him in court. Maya was very frightened to tell the truth because Mr. Freeman had told her he would kill Bailey if she told anyone he had abused her. But Maya did tell the truth in court, and Mr. Freeman was sentenced to one year in jail. He never served time. Later Maya heard that he had been beaten to death. Maya felt like it was her fault that he died because she had told the truth about him in court. She decided not to talk to anyone else again, as someone else might die. For over a year Maya spoke only to Bailey. Soon she and Bailey were sent back to Stamps to live with Momma.

Maya grew up to be a singer, dancer, and writer. She also became active in civil rights issues working with Dr. Martin Luther King, Jr. But we know her best from her writing. Her best seller, *I Know Why the Caged Bird Sings*, is the honest story of her childhood. Maya's words give us insight and inspiration. Like *On the Pulse of Morning* Maya's writing and poems are "songs...of hope, wisdom, and some just plain laughing out loud."

More on Maya

When Maya is working on her writing, she doesn't want to be disturbed. She locks herself in a room, often a hotel room, and refuses to emerge until the project is done.

Name _____ Date _____

What do you remember from your reading?

Using what you have learned in your reading about Maya Angelou, answer the following questions in complete sentences.

1. For what reason did Maya appeal to the people of the United States to come together in unity?

   _____

   _____

2. Why were Maya's memories of living with Momma happy?

   _____

3. Why did Maya not speak for over a year?

   _____

4. What is the name of Maya's autobiography?

   _____

5. Choose the correct word to fill in each blank.

frightened	watching	hypnotic	cadence	insight
inauguration	sentenced	unity	occasion	exchange

a. The magician's medal was _____ as it swung back and forth before his eyes.

b. This poetry has a very uneven _____ .

c. People should come together in _____ to obtain world peace.

d. The dance took place at the _____ , when the President was sworn in.

e. That woman had great _____ to quickly realize what was happening.

Research

Maya Angelou has written other works in addition to her autobiography and *On the Pulse of Morning*. Name at least 5 of them. You may need to consult resource materials to find your answers.

Famous African Americans 5-6, SV 6792-1

Write Poetry

There are many different types of poetry. Some are easy to write, and some are difficult. Poems called sonnets are difficult to write. They must have a certain number of lines, a precise rhyme scheme, and certain meter, or rhythm. Other poems don't really have any rules to follow and are called free-form poetry. One type of poetry that is halfway between these two types of poetry and is fun to write is called a limerick.

A limerick is a nonsense poem, but it has a definite pattern. The limerick has only five lines. The rhyme scheme is "aabba," which means the first, second, and last lines must all end with the same sound or rhyme with one another. The third and fourth lines must end with a different sound that rhymes.

Limericks are fun to write and say and can become very silly. Legend has it that years ago this type of poetry was sung at parties in Ireland. Each person created his own limerick and when he finished, the crowd would yell to the next person, "Will you come up to Limerick?" The nights were filled with laughter and silliness. An example of a limerick that may have been said is:

> There was an old Man of the Dee
> Who was sadly annoyed by a flea;
> When he said, "I will scratch it!"
> They gave him a hatchet
> Which grieved that Old Man of the Dee.

Write your own limerick.

It must have five lines. The first, second, and last lines must end with the same sound or rhyme. The third and fourth lines must rhyme too, but with different sounds. Let this be a fun and silly exercise for you. Have a good time writing this form of poetry.

_____

_____

_____

_____

_____

One Step More

Perhaps your teacher will allow you and your classmates to read your limericks as they did at Irish parties. Be sure to say in unison after each, "Will you come up to Limerick?"

Alex Haley
Writer

Alex Haley sat through the third night, naked, on a wooden board in the hold of a transatlantic steamer. He wanted to experience some of what his ancestors went through years earlier when they were snatched from their homes and brought to America in the "middle passage" of a slave ship. For several years Alex had been doing grueling research so he could write his book, *Roots: The Saga of an American Family*, which was published in 1976.

Born in Ithaca, New York, Alex was taken by his mother to live with her family in a small town called Henning in Tennessee while his father finished his college degree at Cornell University. Alex lived a happy childhood in the little rural community. He became close to his grandmother and loved listening to her tell of his relatives long ago. Alex sat "scrunched down, listening, behind Grandma's squeaky chair," fascinated. The stories told about Alex's great-great-great-great grandfather, who was brought by slave ship to Annapolis, Maryland, and sold to a plantation master in Spotsylvania County, Virginia. The relative's name was Kin-tay. When he had children, he told them of his home in Africa, and in turn they told their children, so the family history had been passed to each generation.

Alex joined the Coast Guard when he was 17 years old. In his spare time he read constantly and soon began writing stories of his own. For eight years he submitted stories to magazines for publication and eventually got one published. The Coast Guard created a new title for him in 1949—Chief Journalist. Alex retired from the Coast Guard after 20 years of service and dedicated his life to being a full-time freelance writer. It was when he was doing research for one of his stories in the National Archives in Washington, D.C., that he thought of his grandmother's stories of his family. He decided to see if he could find the names of any of his ancestors. He found the names of his mother's great-grandparents. Ignited with curiosity he continued to search in the Archives. This was the beginning of a 12-year period in which he did extensive research. He even traveled by safari to the African village of his ancestors, the Kinte Clan.

Alex's Awards

In 1977 Alex Haley received a special citation from the Pulitzer Prize Board for his book, *Roots: The Saga of an American Family*. That same year he received the Spingarn Medal, an award given to an outstanding African American who has risen to the top of his profession.

In *Roots: The Saga of an American Family*, Alex combined fact and fiction, which he termed "faction," to tell the history of his family, beginning in the 1700s. The book was made into an eight-part dramatization which was on television in 1977. The miniseries, a portrayal of the degradations of slavery, attracted over 130 million viewers, the largest television audience in history. Until his death in 1992, Alex Haley continued his involvement in literary projects.

Name_____ Date_____

What do you remember from your reading?

Using what you have learned from your reading about Alex Haley, answer the following questions in complete sentences.

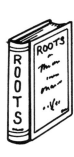

1. Name three ways in which Alex Haley tried to understand and discover more about his family. _____

_____

_____

_____

2. What impact did Alex's grandmother's stories have on his life?

_____

3. What affect did reading have on Alex?

_____

4. Why did the Coast Guard create a new title for Alex Haley?

_____

5. Choose a word from your reading to fit each of the following definitions:

a. spanning or crossing the Atlantic _____

b. persons from whom one is descended _____

c. one who proceeds as an independent _____

d. a journey or trip _____

e. transition from a higher to a lower level of quality_____

Research

Slaves were brought to the United States in ships. This story talks about the "middle passage" of a slave ship. Consult a research book to discover more about the "middle passage" as well as other cruelties that befell slaves. Using your research write the outline for a brief paper about the transportation of slaves to the United States.

Discover Your Roots

Alex Haley worked over 12 years researching his genealogy. His search took him to foreign countries and allowed him to better understand himself. He was able to trace his family's history back to the 1700s. He believed that by knowing a little about our ancestors we are better able to know ourselves.

Complete the branches of your family tree.

The following exercise is one for which you may need to ask your parents' help. Fill in each space with the appropriate name of your relative.

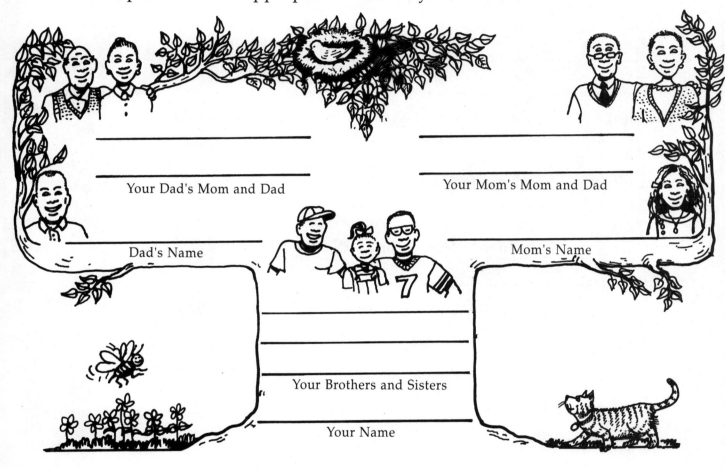

Your Dad's Mom and Dad

Your Mom's Mom and Dad

Dad's Name

Mom's Name

Your Brothers and Sisters

Your Name

One Step More

Next to each name on your family tree, write in an adjective that describes your relative. The adjective could describe the person's temperament, looks, or personality. If you know where the person lived, write that fact, too. From these descriptions you may be able to see from whom you received your own traits.

Branching Out

Can you name any other relatives in generations before your grandparents? Include their names on your family tree, as well.

Famous African Americans 5-6, SV 6792-1

John H. Johnson
Entrepreneur

The 24-year-old African American walked briskly down the Chicago streets, bracing himself against the cold winds blowing fiercely over Lake Michigan. John H. Johnson had recently borrowed $500 and used his mother's furniture as collateral to start a magazine for African Americans. It had never been done and was a very big gamble, but John had "decided once and for all" that he would "make it or die." The first issue of *Negro Digest* was published November 1, 1942.

John and his mother had moved from Arkansas City, Arkansas, "where Blacks could only work as domestics or laborers on the Mississippi River levee," he explained years later. His mother had wanted to move to Chicago so her son, John, could attend high school. There was no high school for African Americans in Arkansas City. John said, "My mother never went beyond the third grade. Yet she was the best-educated person I ever met. She was daring, caring, she believed you could do anything you wanted to do, if you tried. She gave me faith and...hope, and that has guided my life."

John's venture to start a magazine was a long shot. He was very frightened it may not be successful. He wondered how he would pay back the printer and the loan company. But most important he wondered if he would disgrace his mother who had sacrificed so much for him.

Johnson's Journey

On the celebration of his 45th year in business Johnson says, "What a difference 45 years make! On November 1, 1942, I was poor, ambitious, and scared to death. On November 1, 1986, I'm rich, ambitious, and scared to death. That's why I got up at five o'clock this morning. That's why I'm still running. I'm scared somebody will pinch me and wake me up."

When *Negro Digest* hit the magazine stands it was a success, and John was on his way. Years later he recounted how the magazine had opened a "vein of pure black gold." In honor of the month of November when the magazine was first published, John adopted that month as his signature month. Whenever he launched a new business endeavor, he chose November to do it. On November 1, 1945, he began *Ebony* magazine. On November 1, 1951, he started *Jet*. In other Novembers he founded Fashion Fair Cosmetics and Supreme Beauty Products and bought controlling shares in Supreme Life Insurance Company where years before he had begun his career as a "go-fer" and office boy.

He is a man who has risen from the poverty rolls to Forbes magazine's roll of the 400 richest Americans at an estimated worth of over $200 million dollars. He says, "long shots do come in, and...hard work, dedication, and perseverance will overcome almost any prejudice and open almost any door. I believe that the only failure is failing to try."

Name _____ Date _____

What do you remember from your reading?

Using what you have learned from your reading about John Johnson, answer the following questions in complete sentences.

1. How do you know John Johnson was serious about his business venture?

    _____

    _____

2. What sacrifice did his mother make for him? _____

    _____

3. Why was John's idea to start a magazine such a long shot?

    _____

    _____

4. More than luck, what did John say were the reasons for his success?

    _____

    _____

5. Write each word in a sentence in the first person, using your own words.

    Example: *adopted: I adopted that idea as my own.*

    a. collateral _____

    b. domestics _____

    c. venture_____

    d. perseverance _____

    e. prejudice _____

Research

Have you ever read an issue of *Ebony* or *Jet*? Most libraries and newsstands have copies. Select one of the magazines and examine its format. Note any differences or similarities to other magazines you may have read. Why do you think *Jet* and *Ebony* are so popular?

Write a comparison/contrast paragraph in which you compare *Jet* or *Ebony* to another magazine of your choice. Be sure to include a topic sentence and supporting details.

Name _____ Date _____

Develop a Business Plan

When John Johnson was a young man, he had an idea for a business product—a magazine for African Americans. It was unique because there were no other magazines targeted for the African-American market. He researched his idea and knew how much money he needed to get started. Fortunately for John Johnson, his careful planning and good idea worked together to create a successful business.

You can develop a business plan.

There are many opportunities for young adults to be involved in their own businesses. Teenagers have been babysitting and mowing lawns for years. There are other business opportunities for clever teenagers, too.

1. Think of a product or service you could provide for your neighborhood, school, or community. Be creative! _____

    _____

2. How will your product or service be unique from other ones already provided?

    _____

    _____

3. What will be your marketing channels? In other words, how will you let other people know about your product or service?

    _____

    _____

4. Who do you plan to target as your buying market? In other words, who is

    likely to buy your product or service? _____

    _____

5. How much money will you need to get started in your business? (Don't overlook the costs of any flyers or literature you may pass out to advertise your business.)

    _____

6. What price will you charge for your product or service? _____

Toni Morrison
Writer

Toni Morrison had just put her two little boys to bed, snuggled warmly and protected from the harsh Syracuse, New York, winds that howled outside. Now the rest of the evening would be her time. This winter was especially lonely for Toni. She had recently divorced from her husband and had moved to Syracuse to take a job as an editor with Random House. Like so many other nights that winter, Toni sat down at her writing desk to work on a story about a little African-American girl who wanted blue eyes. Writing was a way for Toni to escape the loneliness and depression she felt.

Years before, Toni had been involved with a writers' group that met once a month to read and critique one another's work. Toni once wrote a story about a childhood conversation she had had with another little African-American girl in Ohio. The little girl had told her that she was mad at God because she had prayed for two years for Him to give her blue eyes, but He never did. That conversation had always remained with Toni because it spoke to her about the way African-American children were taught to think about their identities. Although the members of the writing group liked the story, Toni did not do anything with the story after that night. She put it away and nearly forgot about it.

Toni rediscovered the story when she moved to Syracuse in 1967 and decided to expand it into her first novel, *The Bluest Eye*. Toni wanted to do the story for African Americans in the language in which they speak. She wanted it to be about their culture and lives, and she wanted to use the familiar sayings of the African-American people. She said she did not want to have to explain what a particular saying may mean. African Americans would know. Toni felt no other writer was writing this way. She wanted to try something different.

Toni's Title

Toni Morrison was born Chloe, but when she was in college no one could pronounce her name, so she changed it to Toni.

Toni drew upon her childhood experiences in Loraine, Ohio, to develop the characters for her book. The book is about Pecola Breedlove, the girl who wanted blue eyes, and her only friends, Claudia and Frieda McTeer. Pecola is a very sad and lonely girl who believes that if only she had blue eyes, her life would be better. After many late nights of writing, Toni finished her book. It was published in 1969 and was well-received by African Americans and white people alike.

After the publication of *The Bluest Eye*, Toni continued writing other books and plays. She won the Pulitzer Prize for the 1987 book called *Beloved*, a story about a woman who escaped from slavery. In 1993 Toni Morrison received one of the world's highest honors. She became the first African American to win the Nobel Prize in Literature.

What do you remember from your reading?

Using what you have learned from your reading about Toni Morrison, answer the following questions in complete sentences.

1. Why did the childhood conversation with the girl who wanted

    blue eyes have such an impact on Toni? _____

    _____

    _____

2. What was different about Toni's novel, *The Bluest Eye*?

    _____

    _____

3. Why did Pecola Breedlove want blue eyes?_____

    _____

    _____

4. What is the greatest literary award Toni Morrison has received?

    _____

5. Write an original sentence using each of the following words:

   a. editor _____

   b. critique_____

   c. identities _____

   d. culture _____

   e. characters _____

Research

Toni was awarded the Nobel Prize in Literature for her writing. There are other Nobel Prizes, too. Write down all of the ones of which you have heard.

Research the different awards given by the Nobel foundation and explain the purpose of each. How many of the prizes did you name?

Include your findings in complete sentences within a paragraph.

Understand the language

Toni Morrison writes about African-American experiences. Sometimes her writings mean one thing to African Americans and another to white readers. And that's fine. She wants to speak to her audience without having to explain what certain phrases mean.

Often language has double meaning or is symbolic. For instance, when a person says, "It's raining cats and dogs," does he really mean that animals are falling from the sky? Of course not! He means it's raining quite a bit—there are a lot of cats and dogs; there is a lot of rain.

Look at the following sayings and write the meaning of each. None of them literally means what the words say.

1. You can't judge a book by its cover. _____

   _____

2. Don't count your chickens until they hatch._____

   _____

3. Let's hit the road. _____

4. Don't judge someone until you've walked a mile in his shoes.

   _____

   _____

   _____

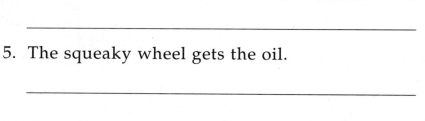

5. The squeaky wheel gets the oil.

   _____

   _____

   _____

6. Don't change horses in the middle of the stream.

   _____

   _____

Famous African Americans 5-6, SV 6792-1

Gordon Parks
Filmmaker, Author, Photographer, Artist

The year was 1942. A young photographer received his first assignment, but it did not involve his camera. He was to purchase a coat, get some lunch, and take in a movie. As he attempted to complete his assignment, he began to discover that Washington, D.C., the city in which he had just taken a job and in which he would live, was not going to be a comfortable place for an African American. He found that he would be able to buy a coat, but he would not be allowed to try one on for size. He would be able to get some lunch, but he would not be allowed to sit down in the restaurant to eat it. At the movie theater, he was not even allowed in the door. He became very angry. This was the reaction his boss expected— and wanted. He knew Gordon Parks had talent. Now he knew Gordon was fired-up to photograph with a purpose. That day Gordon took his most famous photograph, called *American Gothic*, of a custodian named Ella Watson. She worked in his building and had a story of oppression and despair that moved him to place her in front of the American flag with a mop and a broom in her hands, much like the original painting of *American Gothic* in which the farmer and his wife stand with pitchfork in hand in front of their barn.

Parks' Prizes

Gordon Parks has received 28 honorary degrees, and he was given the National Medal of Arts by President Reagan in 1988.

Gordon Parks was no stranger to intolerance or hard times. He was born the youngest of 15 children in 1912. His family's farm in Kansas was a place filled with love and not much more. When his mother died 14 years later, the family split apart.

Over the following years, Gordon's strength came from the love his mother had given him and her words of encouragement which he remembered always. Though he had never finished high school, he taught himself to write and to paint. Before he became interested in photography, he had been a piano player, a basketball player, a woodsman, and a railroad waiter. He read continuously, and he began to write.

The Learning Tree, Gordon's first novel, was published in 1963. The book was based on his childhood experiences, and it became a best-seller. He later made a movie about the book which got mixed reviews, but most critics were impressed by the visual beauty of the film.

Gordon says, "Young people should never accept a limit on their horizons. In fact, older people shouldn't either. A lot of black kids today think it's enough to read black poetry or play black music. But it's not. You should learn where you came from. But don't stop there: Learn everything there is to know." His latest endeavor has been writing a piano sonata for his children. What do you think will be his next venture?

What do you remember from your reading?

Using what you have learned about Gordon Parks from your reading, answer the following questions in complete sentences.

1. What was the nature of Gordon Parks' first assignment as a photographer?

   _____

   _____

2. Why was Gordon unable to see a movie in Washington, D.C.?

   _____

   _____

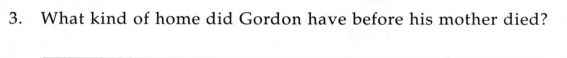

3. What kind of home did Gordon have before his mother died?

   _____

4. What was Gordon's first movie called, and what was it about?

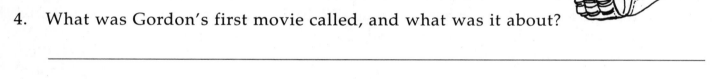

   _____

   _____

5. Find one *synonym* for each of the following words:

   a. reaction _____

   b. oppression _____

   c. intolerance _____

   d. encouragement _____

   e. endeavor _____

Research

Gordon Parks has written about ten books, including *The Learning Tree.* Find out the names of three of his other books and write a sentence or two about each one. You will not need to read every book to write your sentences. Think about where you can find this information.

Name_____ Date_____

Make an Outline

Before writing a story, it is usually a good idea to put your ideas down on paper. One good method is to make an outline. A well-organized outline can make your writing much quicker, easier, and better.

Let's say that you, like Gordon Parks, wish to write a story about your own life. What events stand out in your life? Think of them in chronological order—from the time you were born until today.

First, give the big events in your life a Roman numeral. For example:

I. Birth

This big event, your birth, will form the **title sentence** for your first paragraph.

Second, break each big event down into smaller happenings. Continuing the example of birth, your outline could continue this way:

I. Birth
    a. When Mom found out she was going to have a baby.
    b. What happened on the way to the hospital.
    c. My weight and length.

These lettered items will build the **body of your paragraph**(s) about your birth.

Third, these smaller happenings can be broken down even further. You could talk to your mother and find out what she did when she found out she was going to have a baby. Maybe something happened on the way to the hospital. This information would appear in your outline like this:

    I. Birth
        a. When Mom found out she was going to have a baby.
            1. She called her mother.
            2. Dad didn't believe her at first.
        b. What happened on the way to the hospital.
            1. Dad went through a red light and was stopped by a policeman.
            2. The policeman gave Mom and Dad an escort to the hospital!

Continue on with the larger events in your life, giving each one a Roman numeral. Break them all down into smaller pieces. Ask your family for details you may not remember about things that happened when you were younger. Remember to write in complete sentences. When you are finished, your story will be easy and fun to write. Your well-organized notes will help you to write a clear, entertaining story that your classmates and your family will enjoy!

Name_____ Date_____

Unit I Review
Maya Angelou, Alex Haley, John Johnson, Toni Morrison, Gordon Parks

Write the answers to the following questions using complete sentences.

1. What did Maya Angelou mean when she said she wanted to write

   in a new way?_____

   _____

2. What did Alex Haley do to prepare himself for the writing of *Roots*?

   _____

   _____

3. What steps did John Johnson take to begin his first business venture?

   _____

   _____

4. Where did Toni Morrison get the idea for her book, *The Bluest Eye*?

   _____

   _____

5. What did Gordon Parks experience on his first day of work as a photographer

   in Washington, D.C.? _____

   _____

6. Use each of the following words in sentences: insight, ancestors, perseverence, culture, and endeavor.

   _____

   _____

   _____

   _____

   _____

7. Write a brief paragraph about the way writing, or the printed word, played a part in the lives of each person in this unit. Use the back of this paper or a separate sheet.

Kenneth "Babyface" Edmonds
Musician

"Whitney, I just want you to hear this one song. If you like it, you'll do it," said Kenneth ("Babyface") Edmonds, to the superstar, Whitney Houston. Whitney did not want to sing on the soundtrack of *Waiting to Exhale*. Babyface started playing the song on the piano, just the melody because he hadn't written the lyrics yet, and Whitney immediately liked it. She started helping make up lyrics, "Count on me through thick and thin/ A friendship that will never end..." Babyface's music had again won over a superstar. They recorded *Count on Me* as well as two more songs. Babyface wrote and produced the soundtrack for *Waiting to Exhale* which included Whitney's hit, *Count on Me*, and it sold over seven million copies.

The musically self-taught Babyface was born in Indianapolis, Indiana. In 1982 he was in a pop band called The Deele when he met Antonio ("L.A.") Reid, a man who became his longtime business associate and songwriting partner. The two wrote hit songs for The Whispers and Bobby Brown in the late 1980s. Although Babyface and L.A. don't write songs together anymore, they jointly operate the record company, LaFace.

In 1989, Babyface had his first Rhythm & Blues Number One hit as a solo act with the song, *It's No Crime.* From there his career took off—primarily in writing and producing hits for other artists. Clive Davis, of Artista Records, says of Babyface, "He brings something special out of the artists who interpret his material. He writes different ways for different people." Babyface has written hits for Whitney Houston, Toni Braxton, Michael Jackson, Boyz II Men, Mariah Carey, Eric Clapton, and Madonna. By the end of 1996, he had written and produced more than 100 top 10 R&B hits, 16 of which were Number One hits. He wrote two hits for Boyz II Men that joined the ranks of the all-time biggest chart-toppers.

> ## Babyface Says
>
> "For me, it's about being in a good mood to sing... If I don't feel it, I don't stay in the studio."

Still Babyface is soft spoken and modest of his accomplishments. "A genius is Stevie Wonder. A genius is Prince. Those kind of artists, they have no choice. They have to write. I'm just a song man." The song man, Babyface, believes he has room for growth. "I'm just getting to the point right now where I think I can really do something. I've been very blessed to have hits and some good songs here and there, but when I look at songs from Stevie Wonder, from the Beatles—great, great songs—I know I'm still trying to do those great things. I feel like I'm in the process of growing." His music is influenced by his many experiences. While he leans more toward R&B, a lot of his work is rock. He says, "Today's music is so integrated, you can go a lot of places at this point."

Regardless of the direction he ultimately takes, the soft, gentle style of the melodies Babyface has produced will go down as one of the signature styles of his time.

     Famous African Americans 5-6, SV 6792-1

What do you remember from your reading?

Using what you have learned about Kenneth "Babyface" Edmonds from your reading, answer the following questions in complete sentences.

1. How did Babyface persuade Whitney Houston to sing on the soundtrack of *Waiting to Exhale*?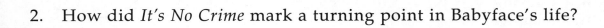
_____

2. How did *It's No Crime* mark a turning point in Babyface's life?

_____

_____

3. What producing success had Babyface enjoyed up until 1996?

_____

4. How does Babyface regard himself as a song writer?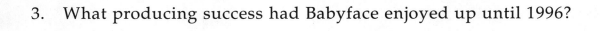

_____

5. Choose another word from your reading that means the same as the bold word(s) in each sentence.

   a. The **tune** of the song was very pretty. _____

   b. The **words** to that song are difficult to remember. _____

   c. He had a been a **partner** of mine for a long time. _____

   d. It took them some time to **figure out the meaning** of the note._____

   e. She was **not one to brag** about the things she had done. _____

Research

By 1996 Babyface had released four solo albums. What is the name of the last album he released in 1996?

_____

Write Song Lyrics

Writing lyrics to a song can be a lot of fun. Sometimes a songwriter will have the music written and know the way he wants the words to sound (melody), but he will need to fill in with the lyrics, or words.

Now you are a songwriter.

The music or tune for your song has been written, now you will write the words. The tune you will be using is the same as the tune for the song, *Kookaburra.*

Just in case you have forgotten the lyrics, they are written here for you. Although you can't use the same words, these will help you with the cadence and rhyme of your lyrics. Counting words and syllables on a line may help you too.

1. Kookaburra sits in the old gum tree,
    Eating all the gumdrops he can see.
    Wait, Kookaburra!
    Wait, Kookaburra!
    Leave some there for me.

Write your lyrics on the following lines. Write at least two verses for your song.

1. _____

_____

_____

_____

2. _____

_____

_____

_____

Sing it again, Sam

Once the class has finished their tunes, divide into groups and share them with one another. Pick the best ones to sing aloud to the class.

Bill Cosby
Comedian/Actor

There are few Americans today who do not recognize the smiling face of William Henry Cosby, Jr. He stars in his own television shows, sells us pudding, appears on the covers of his over 27 comedy albums, delights us with the books he has written, shows up in the movies, and hosts his own cartoon series, *Fat Albert and the Cosby Kids*. But it wasn't always so.

In the early 1960s, Bill was attending Temple University in Philadelphia. He worked nights as a bartender, serving jokes along with people's orders. The regulars at the club got to know Bill as an entertaining young man. One night, the club's regular act did not appear, and Bill's boss asked if he would step in and perform his act for the customers. That turned out to be just the first of many nights that Bill entertained at clubs. The customers loved his act; Bill was a natural. He liked it so much and was so successful, in fact, that he dropped out of Temple to be a full-time entertainer.

Bill was born in Philadelphia in 1937. In his life he has accomplished so much, but he has not always done things in conventional ways. He dropped out of high school to become a medic in the Navy. While in the Navy, Bill finished his studies and got his high school diploma. After he left the Navy, Bill went to Temple University. Though he dropped out of Temple, too, he again finished his education later. He returned to college and got a bachelor's degree. Later Bill went to the University of Massachusetts and earned a master's degree and a doctorate in education in 1977, when he was 39 years old.

Bill's humor is always gentle and never makes us laugh at another person's expense. When listening to Bill Cosby, we learn to laugh at ourselves and the funny things that happen to everyone at one time or another. He talks about families and the wonder and humor of childhood. It is easy for all people to identify with the stories that Bill tells. That is why he is one of America's most-loved comedians, why he has been loved for so many years, and why his humor will last for many, many years to come.

Bits on Bill

Bill was the first African-American actor to star in a network television series. It was called *I Spy*.

When Bill came up with his idea for *The Cosby Show*, most people thought it would not work. They thought a show about an everyday family with everyday problems would be boring. *The Cosby Show* lasted for eight years!

Famous African Americans 5–6, SV 6792-1

What do you remember about Bill Cosby?

Using what you have learned about Bill Cosby from your reading, answer the questions below using complete sentences.

1. How do you know Bill Cosby's show about everyday people was

   popular? _____

   _____

2. Name at least six occupations Bill has had in his life.

   _____

   _____

3. Why do so many people enjoy Bill Cosby's kind of humor?

   _____

   _____

4. What did Bill do to demonstrate the importance of education in his life?

   _____

5. Find a word in your reading that has a similar meaning to the word(s) in bold type.

a. The soldier called for the **field doctor** when he was wounded. _____

b. That is not the **established** way that we do things. _____

c. He worked very hard to get his **doctor's degree**. _____

d. She has a wonderful **sense of the comical**. _____

e. I could really **affiliate myself** with that story. _____

Research

Bill had three degrees by the time he left the University of Massachusetts. Think about what you would like to do when you graduate. What kind of degree might you need for the occupation you choose? If you were to continue your education past a Bachelor's degree, what would your next step be? And the next? Write a paragraph describing your choice and the education necessary to reach your goal.

Name_____ Date_____

Share Your Findings

Bill Cosby has done so many different things. Find a book he has written, a movie he has been in, or a record he has made. Do a report and create a piece of art to describe what you read or see to the rest of your class.

You may use this paper to write your report. If you need more space, use another sheet of paper or the back of this one.

1. What is the name of the movie, book, or record? _____
    _____

2. If it is a movie, when was it made? If it is a book, when was it published, and by whom? If it is a record, when was it recorded?
    _____

3. Who are the other actors in the movie? Who are the principle characters in the book? Who are the people on the record?
    _____
    _____

4. What is the movie about? What is the book about? What happens on the record?
    _____
    _____

6. What is your favorite part? _____
    _____
    _____

7. How did watching, reading, or listening to Bill Cosby make you feel?
    _____
    _____

8. Why would you recommend this experience to your classmates?
    _____
    _____

The artwork you create to go with this report may be of your choosing. You may draw or paint a picture, make a collage, use papier maché, build a model, use clay, or any other medium with which you enjoy working. Have fun!

Whoopi Goldberg
Actress

In the 1985 film production of Alice Walker's novel, *The Color Purple*, director Steven Spielberg cast a newcomer to the big screen in the lead roll of Celie, a victim of spousal abuse. The actress had made a name for herself in theater but had never worked in film, so the choice was a bit of a gamble. The film opened to mixed reviews and much controversial discussion, but the actress who played the lead roll was unforgettable. Whoopi Goldberg won a Golden Globe Award, the NAACP Image Award, and an Academy Award nomination for her portrayal of Celie. Moviegoers everywhere were talking about the "new face" they had seen in *The Color Purple*.

Whoopi was born Caryn Johnson in 1955 in New York City. She lived with her mother, Emma Johnson, and brother, Clyde, in a housing project in the Chelsea section of Manhattan, New York. Emma had to work many different jobs to support her family. In school Whoopi had a problem reading and was sometimes unable to grasp the subject matter. She in fact had dyslexia, a disorder which interfered with her achievement. Whoopi had a fine memory and demonstrated a talent for acting at an early age. When she was about eight years old, her mother enrolled her in a nearby children's theater workshop called the Helena Rubenstein Children's Theatre at the Hudson Guild. She proved to be a talented actress. Over the years she played small roles in Broadway plays.

Whoopi had a brief marriage in the early 1970s, and from it came her daughter, Alexandrea. In 1974 Whoopi needed a change in her life, so she and her daughter moved to the West Coast where she could pursue her childhood ambition to act. "Acting is the one thing I always knew I could do," says Goldberg. This is the time in her life when she started using her stage name, Whoopi Goldberg. Life was difficult for the two in San Diego. Whoopi had to work several different jobs to make ends meet. She was once a bricklayer, as well as a hair stylist at a mortuary. At one point Whoopi and Alexandrea had to go on welfare but were soon able to get off. "Getting off welfare was a sweet triumph," revealed Whoopi.

After her success in *The Color Purple*, Whoopi was cast in several movies that did not do very well. Then came the movie *Ghost*, for which she won an Academy Award as best supporting actress. Since then, Whoopi has played a variety of characters in a number of movies, some successful, some not so successful. Overall she says her main purpose for being an entertainer is to make people laugh. Whoopi Goldberg's rise to stardom has not been an easy one. She's overcome dyslexia, poverty, and divorce to become one of today's most popular entertainers.

Whoopi's Wardrobe

Whoopi says she likes to wear casual clothes when she's out, because it's important for her to be comfortable around her fans. They want to shake her hand and touch her hair. She notes that if you are "in uncomfortable clothes it can make you real crabby."

What do you remember from your reading?

Use the clues to complete the crossword puzzle.

DOWN

1. Whoopi's given first name
2. Clothes Whoopi wears
3. Whoopi's first film
4. Whoopi acted in ___ before making movies
5. To cast Whoopi in *The Color Purple* was a gamble ___ she had never acted in a film.

ACROSS

6. Movie for which Whoopi won Academy Award for Best Supporting Actress
7. Whoopi's reading disorder
8. Whoopi was ___ when she first demonstrated she could act.
9. "New face" actress in *The Color Purple*
10. Whoopi once worked as one
11. Whoopi enjoys making people do this

12. On a separate sheet of paper, write one question that you could ask Whoopi Goldberg using each of the following words:

a. spousal

b. controversial

c. dyslexia

d. pursue

e. ambition

Research

Dyslexia is a common reading disorder. A person can suffer from it for years before it is correctly diagnosed. Consult the encyclopedia or other research materials to find more information on dyslexia. Can you name other Hollywood or political personalities who have dyslexia?

Using your research, write an explanatory paragraph to report your findings. Be sure to include a topic sentence with supporting details.

Retell a Story

Like many other famous entertainers, Whoopi Goldberg draws upon her life experiences to recreate the characters she plays and we enjoy so much. When she has to act sad, she thinks of a sad time in her life. She recreates the emotions she felt at this time and gives them to the character she is playing. This makes her acting believable to us. Conversely, when she must play a scene where she has to be happy and funny, she thinks about a time in her life when she laughed a great deal. When she thinks about this happy time, she is happy and her character appears so, too.

You are the actor.

You are now a famous actor. You have just been cast in what will be the film of the year. It will be a blockbuster hit, and you are the star. Your part calls for you to recreate many different emotions. You will have to act happy, excited, nervous, afraid, and serious. Pick just one of the emotions you will be recreating on film, and write about an experience in your life that you could use to get into character.

_____

_____

_____

_____

_____

_____

_____

_____

_____

_____

_____

_____

_____

_____

Whitney Houston
Singer/Actress

Imagine acting in a hit movie that made $411 million at box offices around the world. Imagine singing in that movie and having your songs break music records. Imagine the soundtrack from that movie selling one million copies in one week! Now imagine that you almost didn't even make that movie! That's how it was for Whitney Houston.

Early in the 1990s Kevin Costner, an actor and director, had an idea for a new movie he was going to direct. The star of the movie was to be named Rachel Marron. She would be a popular singer whose life becomes endangered by a fan. Rachel would hire a bodyguard named Frank Farmer to protect her. Kevin would play the part of Frank Farmer, an ex-Secret Service man, and he wanted Whitney to be Rachel Marron. The name of the movie was to be *The Bodyguard*.

By this time Whitney had already produced three successful albums. She had become the only musician ever to have seven number-one singles in a row. She had won an Emmy Award and a Grammy Award for her song, *Saving All My Love for You*. Her first album, *Whitney Houston*, had sold 18 million copies worldwide. That turned out to be the all-time best-selling first record for a solo artist!

In spite of all her accomplishments, Whitney was nervous about starring in a movie. She thought she should start with smaller parts and work her way around to the starring roles. Though the idea of acting and singing did intrigue her, Whitney hesitated to accept Kevin's offer. But Kevin was persistent. He wanted Whitney for the role, so he waited two years for her to decide. Finally, he called her up, saying, "Are you going to do this movie with me or what?" With Kevin's reassurance that he would help Whitney and that she would do well, she finally agreed to make the movie.

The result was a movie and soundtrack that amazed everyone. The critics did not like *The Bodyguard*, but the movie-going public did. And the music did even better than the movie. It won 11 trophies for Whitney at the 1993 Billboard Music Awards, three Grammys at the 1994 Grammy awards, and favorite album at the 1994 American Music Awards.

Whitney has been surrounded by music since she was a child in New Jersey listening to her mother sing in the church choir and with a gospel group. She has always known that singing is in her soul. Now she has added acting to her talents, and a family to her busy schedule. But Whitney says she will never stop performing. To the people who wonder, Whitney says, "Tell 'em that Whitney Houston still loves entertaining as much as she did when she was nineteen. And she probably still will when she's 99."

Whitney's World

Whitney has many family members working in her production company, Nippy, Inc. She admits sometimes they can get on each other's nerves, but family is what matters the most. Having a close family has helped Whitney deal with the pressures and consequences of being famous.

What do you remember from your reading?

Using what you have learned about Whitney Houston from your reading, answer the questions below in complete sentences.

1. Why didn't Whitney want to make a movie with Kevin Costner?

_____

_____

2. What tells about the success of *The Bodyguard* ? _____

_____

3. What made Whitney realize that she wanted to be a singer?_____

_____

4. What does Whitney say is good and bad about working with her family?

_____

5. Write a brief answer to each question.

a. Name something that is *endangered.*_____

b. What would *intrigue* you about being an actor or actress?_____

c. How would someone act who was being *persistent*?_____

d. What kind of *reassurance* would you want before bungee jumping?

_____

e. Name one of the *consequences* of breaking the law. _____

Research

Write a page-long report about your favorite movie. Answer the following questions in your writing: Who was in the movie? Where did it take place? Name the director and the producer. In what year did the movie come out? What were the main events that shaped the movie? What was your favorite part? Why did you like the movie?

Name_____ Date_____

Advertise a Product

Many companies choose famous stars or sports personalities to help them advertise their products. The famous person can get people's attention, and give people the idea that this is a product that they would like to use. You have probably seen commercials in which Bill Cosby promotes desserts, or Michael Jordan helps sell tennis shoes.

You make the commercial.

Let's say you have a product that you would like Whitney Houston to help you promote. Let's assume that she has agreed to work with you. What kind of product do you think Whitney would use? Think about what your product might be, and how Whitney might help you with your sales.

1. What is your product? _____

2. What does your product do? _____

3. Who will use your product? _____

4. What would be the best way to reach your audience; i.e. television, radio, or internet? _____

5. Why do you think this way is best for your audience?

    _____

    _____

6. What could Whitney do or say that would help your product sell?

    _____

    _____

7. Write a brief description of your commercial or advertisement. Describe what people will do or say, and how your product will be introduced. Tell why your pitch will make people more likely to buy your product than someone else's similar product. Television and radio commercials generally last about 30 seconds. Keep this in mind as you develop your ad.

    _____

    _____

    _____

    _____

Leontyne Price
Opera Singer

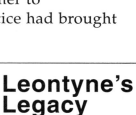

The audience sat spellbound. The stage was set for the Italian opera, *Il Trovatore*. The actors all sang their parts, but one stood out from the rest. The singer who was playing the part of Leonora had a voice that was captivating. It would even be called perfect.

When she finished singing, the audience rose to its feet and began to clap. They continued to fill the Metropolitan Opera House in New York with applause for 42 minutes. The singer had just received the longest ovation in the history of the opera company.

That singer was Leontyne Price. She had been singing since she was just two years old. Her parents, her teachers, and her friends had all helped her to get the training and education she would need to be a success. Years of practice had brought her to where she was that day.

Leontyne Price was born in Laurel, Mississippi in 1927. When she was just two, a music teacher noticed that Leontyne already had some talent for music. Her mother was determined to do all she could to further Leontyne's abilities. A couple of years later, Leontyne had her first piano—though it was a toy piano—and she began her lessons.

Leontyne did not choose music first for a career. She decided to be a teacher, and went to college to get her degree. She continued to include music in her studies, however, and by her last year, her teachers were urging her to keep singing. She was persuaded to apply for a music scholarship and was awarded one at the Juilliard School of Music in New York City. It was a bittersweet time for Leontyne, however. Although she had won the scholarship, she did not have enough money to afford the rest of the costs of attending the school. Fortunately for Leontyne, the Chisholms, family friends, wanted to help. They made it possible for Leontyne to continue her musical career. For that Leontyne has remained thankful throughout her life.

Leontyne soon began performing in operas and her voice and acting was praised by music critics. With her performance in *Tosca*, she became the first African American to appear in a televised opera. In 1959 Leontyne appeared in Vienna in the opera *Aida*, making her an international star.

In 1964 President Johnson awarded Leontyne the Freedom Medal. This is the highest honor a citizen of the United States can receive. President Johnson said, "Her singing has brought light to her land." Leontyne loves singing. She says, "You must like what you are doing if you want to be happy and successful." This is a good thing to remember, coming from the woman with "the golden voice."

Leontyne's Legacy

In 1982 Leontyne opened the convention of The Daughters of the American Revolution in Constitution Hall with a concert honoring Marian Anderson. Marian Anderson had been barred from appearing there by the DAR in 1939 because they did not want an African American to perform. Because of this, President Roosevelt's wife, Eleanor, had angrily quit the organization.

Famous African Americans 5–6, SV 6792-1

What do you remember from your reading?

Using what you have learned from your reading about Leontyne Price, answer the following questions in complete sentences.

1. What was special about the applause that Leontyne received

    for *Il Trovatore*? _____

    _____

2. Leontyne was planning to be a teacher. What made her change her mind?

    _____

3. Why was Leontyne concerned when she won the scholarship to Juilliard School

    of Music? _____

4. Leontyne's appearance in *Tosca* brought about what first?

    _____

5. Use the following five words to write a short paragraph in your own words,
    using complete sentences, about Leontyne Price.

    captivating   applause   ovation   scholarship   persuaded

    _____

    _____

    _____

    _____

    _____

Research

Leontyne has performed in many operas. Name four other operas in which she has performed. Also, name two other famous African-American opera singers.

Explore Sound

Sound is made by the vibration of an object. A singer like Leontyne produces her music through the vibration of her larynx, a part of the throat. The vocal cords are stretched across the larynx. When a person sings or speaks, air rushes from the lungs past the vocal chords, causing them to vibrate. The tighter the vocal chords are, the higher the sound is.

Think about other things in your world that make sound. You can probably guess how animals, instruments, and machines makes sounds, but what about something like the wind? How does the wind "howl?" Why do we hear thunder? Perhaps you will find the answers to these questions when you do the following research.

Research an Instrument

Choose a musical instrument on which to do research. Write about how the instrument produces sound. Be specific in your writing, and use complete sentences.

_____

_____

_____

_____

Illustrate Your Research

Draw a picture to demonstrate the way the instrument you chose to research produces sound. Label the parts of the instrument and clearly show the action that causes the sound we hear.

Oprah Winfrey
Entertainer

Heads turned at the Academy Awards celebration as Oprah Winfrey appeared on stage in a beautiful satin Gianfranco Ferre gown. Her neck and ears were adorned with a stunning diamond necklace and earrings. She laughed and said, "A lot of people offered to lend me jewelry for the night, but I didn't need it, honey—I got my own!" This is typical Oprah. She is warm, funny, and approachable. These qualities, together with a keen sense of self and determination, have taken Oprah to the pinnacle of the entertainment industry.

Things weren't always easy for Oprah, who was born January 29, 1954, in Kosciusko, Mississippi. Her parents were never married and soon went their separate ways to different cities. For the first six years of her life, Oprah lived on a small farm with her paternal grandmother, a strong, religious woman. Oprah was taken to church often, and there her exceptional speaking abilities became evident as early as the age of three.

Soon her mother, Vernita, sent for Oprah to come live with her in Milwaukee, Wisconsin. Things didn't work out well, so Oprah was sent to live with her father, Vernon, in Nashville, Tennessee. For the next three years, the child was sent back and forth between parents, but she finally ended up living with her mother in Milwaukee. She felt neglected by her mother, and she alleges that during this time she was the victim of abuse. Oprah sought refuge in books and her studies at school.

Oh, Oprah!

In addition to hosting daily talk shows, Oprah is an actress, too. She has been seen in several films: *Native Son*, *The Women of Brewster Place*, *Listen Up: The Lives of Quincy Jones*, *There Are No Children Here*, and *The Color Purple*, for which she won an Academy Award Nomination.

When she was 14, Oprah was sent once more to live with her father. Vernon was very strict with her and expected only the best behavior and academic performance. He was in charge, and Oprah knew it. In this environment the adolescent flourished. She was a good student and soon became an award-winning speaker. She even won a scholarship to Tennessee State University.

During her sophomore year in college, Oprah worked as a news anchor for a station in Nashville. She was not only the first woman, but also the first African American, to hold such a position. Oprah continued to accept new assignments and jobs with different stations. Then one day a call came that changed her life. She was asked to host a talk show called "A.M. Chicago" which would compete with "Phil Donahue," a well-established favorite in the area. Soon Oprah's show took off and quickly outdistanced the competition. Within two years, "The Oprah Winfrey Show" was watched by over 10 million people every day. By 1995 she had won six best-talk-show-host Emmys and she had been inducted into the Television Academy Hall of Fame. Forbes magazine says she ranks among the highest paid entertainers in the world. Oprah says, "I wouldn't trade places with anybody. I love getting paid, but I'd do this for free if I had to. Doing talk shows is like breathing to me."

What do you remember from your reading?

Using what you have learned from your reading about Oprah Winfrey, answer the following questions in complete sentences.

1. How did church play an important part in Oprah's young childhood?

    _____

    _____

2. Why did Oprah read and study so much when she was young?

    _____

    _____

3. Why did Oprah flourish in her father's home? _____

    _____

4. What telephone call changed Oprah's life? _____

    _____

5. Write a synonym for each of the following words:

    a. adorned _____

    b. pinnacle _____

    c. refuge _____

    d. academic _____

    e. adolescent _____

Research

Oprah Winfrey is well known for her generosity. She splurges on lavish gifts for her friends, including a million dollar home to her best friend, Gayle Bumpus. She gives to many organizations as well.

Utilize the resources in your library to discover what or who else benefits from Oprah's generosity. Write your findings in the form of a report. Be sure to include specific donations/gifts and recipients. Include dates if you can find them.

Interview a Person From History

Oprah Winfrey is famous for her talk show. She regularly interviews celebrities and gets them to talk openly with her as if they were close friends. Before a show Oprah has to do her homework. She prepares the questions she will ask, keeping in mind the direction she wishes the show to go. Sometimes she takes her show on the road. She leaves her cozy studio in Chicago and cruises America, stopping in cities where events are happening to shape history.

You are the Talk Show Host

You have won a contest where you will be the guest host on Oprah's talk show. This is a very special show because you will be able to interview anyone you wish. The person can be historical or contemporary. You may choose someone who is no longer living. You will need to do your homework just like Oprah. You will need to decide where the show will take place, and you will need a list of 10 questions to ask the person. The purpose of your show will be to introduce the viewing audience to the person you are interviewing. You will want to discover a little about the person's character and what important events have taken place in the person's life.

1. Which person will you interview? _____

2. Why did you choose this person? _____

    _____

3. Where will you tape the show? _____

4. Why did you select this location? _____

5. What do you want your audience to learn about this person from your show?

    _____

    _____

6. List 3-4 key questions you will ask this person to make sure your show accomplishes its purpose.

    1. _____

    2. _____

    3. _____

    4. _____

Name _____ Date _____

Unit 2 Review
Babyface, Bill Cosby, Whoopi Goldberg, Whitney Houston, Leontyne Price, Oprah Winfrey

Write the answers to the following questions using complete sentences.

1. What makes Babyface's music stand out from other musicians' music? _____

2. How did Bill Cosby get his start in the entertainment industry?

   _____

3. What problem does Whoopi Goldberg have that interfered with her achievements in school? _____

4. Why would someone as successful as Whitney Houston be nervous about starring in a movie? _____

5. Why was it a bittersweet time for Leontyne Price when she was accepted into Juilliard School of Music? _____

6. How does Oprah Winfrey feel about her job as a television talk-show hostess?

   _____

7. Write a brief answer for each of the following:

   a. Write a line of **lyrics** from your favorite song. _____

   b. When might you want a **medic** with you? _____

   c. What is your **ambition** in life? _____

   d. What might be the **consequences** of lying to a friend? _____

   e. What must you do to be eligible for a **scholarship**? _____

   f. Name the opposite of **pinnacle**. _____

8. What statement could you make that would be true for all of the people studied in this unit?

   _____

Tom Bradley
Politician

Tom Bradley was in his senior year of college at U.C.L.A. Although athletics had been his ticket to a scholarship, his studies were his first priority because he wanted to attend law school. He knew his grades had to be very good in order to be accepted into law school. One day some of his friends invited him to go with them to take the exam to be a police officer. Tom knew he needed a way to support himself in law school, so he took the test and passed. When he graduated from college, Tom joined the police force. He explains, "I joined the police force because of my desire to serve the city which had given me so much." Over the next 50 years Tom Bradley continued serving the city of Los Angeles in the way of public service.

Thomas Bradley was born in Calvert, Texas, on December 29, 1917. His parents were sharecroppers on a cotton plantation. Although they worked long, hard hours, the family was still very poor. Often Tom had to go to bed at night hungry because there wasn't enough food for everyone. Wanting a better life for themselves, the family moved to California where Mr. Bradley found work as a railroad porter, and Mrs. Bradley worked as a domestic. His parents worked very long hours so Tom found himself, at the age of 7, the head of the household. Tom's parents gave him faith that there was a better life to come if he was willing to work for it. He knew it would come to him, and he wasn't afraid to go after it.

> ## Tom's Trophies
>
> In 1982 Democrat Tom Bradley became the first African American nominated by a major party as a candidate for governor.

Although Tom completed law school at Southwestern University Law School in 1956, he stayed with the police force for 21 years, becoming the first African American to achieve the rank of lieutenant. After his retirement in 1960, he did practice law for several years. But the desire to serve his city again began to nag at him. With the help of the African-American community, Tom ran for City Council in 1963, and won the seat, becoming the first African American to sit on the Los Angeles City Council.

Tom Bradley was able to work with all people, bringing them together to get a job done. In 1973 he decided to run for Mayor of Los Angeles. Never before had an African American held this office. In fact only 15 percent of the voters in Los Angeles were African American. Tom and his supporters worked very hard. "If you simply say, 'That can't be done!' and you don't try, how will you ever know?" believed Tom. He won the election. The people of Los Angeles put much faith in him as their leader and re-elected him at every mayoral election until his retirement as Mayor in 1992. Tom Bradley's life has been one of service to others. He has become one of America's most admired and respected politicians.

Name_____ Date_____

What do you remember from your reading?

Using what you have learned in your reading about Tom Bradley, answer the following questions in complete sentences.

1. How did Tom Bradley pay for his undergraduate degree at U.C.L.A.?

   _____

   _____

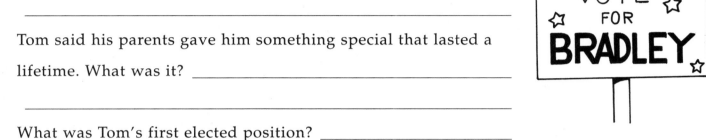

2. Tom said his parents gave him something special that lasted a

   lifetime. What was it? _____

   _____

3. What was Tom's first elected position? _____

   _____

4. What was so unusual about Tom's winning the mayoral election?

   _____

5. Find a word from your reading that has the same meaning as the word(s) in bold type.

   a. Tom Bradley's parents were **people who worked the land and gave part of their crop to the landlord.**

      _____

   b. Serving his city became Tom's **item of prior importance.** _____

   c. Tom's life has been devoted to **community** service._____

   d. Tom's father was a **person who waited on passengers** on trains. _____

   e. One of the gifts Tom's parents gave him was a strong **belief** in good things to come.

      _____

Research

1. Tom and his wife are a good team. They were childhood sweethearts and best

   friends. What is her name? _____

2. How has she helped Tom over the years? _____

   _____

   _____

Campaign for Office

In his lifetime Tom Bradley campaigned for public office many times. It was important for him to know the people he would serve—their problems, concerns, and desires for a better city. He was an exceptional campaigner because he seemed to have his finger on the pulse of the people.

You are the candidate.

Your school has decided to elect a president and you are a candidate. Before election day you will need to develop a campaign and a platform on which to run. There is only a short time before election day, so you need to get started.

Issues: What are three issues facing your school that you think need changing?

1. _____

2. _____

3. _____

Platform: How would you address these issues (from above) or make them better?

1. _____

2. _____

3. _____

Candidate: What characteristics do you have that would make you a good president?

1. _____

2. _____

3. _____

On the Campaign Trail

Now that you have established the issues facing your school and how you will handle them, you will need to develop a slogan and campaign materials. You will want to incorporate some of your characteristics into your materials.

What clever saying could you use for your campaign slogan? Design a campaign button and sign that your classmates will wear and use to rouse support for you. The materials must include more than simply, "Vote for..." and your name.

Shirley Chisholm
United States Representative

Until 1964 Shirley Chisholm had spent the previous 22 years of her life in the field of education. She began with her training at Brooklyn College and her work as a teacher. Later she began working toward her Master's Degree in Early Childhood Education, directed a private nursery school and then a child care center in Manhattan, and finally became educational consultant for New York City's Bureau of Child Welfare.

But Shirley had always wanted to make a difference for her people. Government had always interested her. She wanted to serve the people by getting new laws passed. She wanted them to have better jobs, better places to live, and better schools.

So Shirley became active in politics. She ran for a couple of local posts, but did not win. Then in 1964 Shirley ran for a seat in the New York State Assembly. This time she won, and she began her distinguished career in politics. When Shirley won a seat in the United States Congress in 1968, she became the first African-American woman to hold that position. Her campaign slogan was, "Fighting Shirley Chisholm—Unbought and Unbossed."

Shirley made sure that she got appointments to committees that would allow her to concentrate on the problems that she thought were most important. She became known as a strong fighter for the poor people who had voted for her and whom she was there to represent.

In 1971 Shirley became the first African-American woman to run for President of the United States. She entered the race for the Democratic Party's nomination. Shirley did not really believe she would win. However she did believe that by running, people would take notice. She wanted to draw attention to the fact that there were both women and African Americans who were serious about politics and who wanted to make a difference. She did not win the nomination, but people did take notice.

In 1982 Shirley retired from politics and returned to her first profession. She became a teacher at Mount Holyoke College in Massachusetts. There she shared all she had learned with her students.

Pre-School Politics

Perhaps Shirley Chisholm was destined to be a leader and a policy-maker—at the age of three, she already enjoyed telling other children what to do!

What do you remember from your reading?

Using what you have learned from your reading about Shirley Chisholm, answer the following questions in complete sentences.

1. How many years of Shirley's life were devoted to politics?

   _____

2. Why did Shirley want to enter the field of politics?

   _____

   _____

3. How did Shirley ensure that once she got into politics she would be able to work in the areas that concerned her?

   _____

   _____

4. What were two of Shirley's "firsts" in politics? _____

   _____

   _____

5. Write an original sentence using each of the following words in a different form that the one shown: Example: *active*: <u>*We were actively involved in that group*</u>.

   a. private _____

   b. consultant _____

   c. distinguished _____

   d. campaign_____

   e. nomination _____

Research

You already know that Shirley was honing her leadership abilities early in life. Shirley had some other traits and talents that set her apart from other children at a young age. Do some research on Shirley Chisholm to find out what she was like as a child. Write your findings in a half-page report. Remember to write in complete sentences, and include in your report your source of information.

Apply for a Job

Shirley Chisholm was concerned that the people in her district needed better housing, improved education, and better jobs. When you are ready to begin a job search, you will probably be asked to complete a job application. Applications will vary, but most of them have the same basic components. Fill in the application below for a position as a manager at a retail store. Use your own name and address, but use your imagination to make up other details, such as other positions you have held, money you have earned, responsibilities, and other experiences you have had that make you a good candidate for the job!

Application for Employment
XYZ Company

Name: _____ Date: _____

Address: _____

Birthdate: _____ Position Applied For: _____

Date Available: _____ Will work: P/T _____ F/T _____ W/E _____

Do you have dependable transportation? Yes_____ No _____

Work History: (List your three most recent positions and earnings.)

COMPANY NAME & ADDRESS	DATES TO/FROM	SALARY	RESPONSIBILITIES
1.			
2.			
3.			

Other work experience you believe makes you a strong candidate for the position:

_____

Abilities or skills you believe make you a strong candidate for the position:

_____

List three references (other than relatives) whom we can contact for references. Include addresses, phone numbers, and relationship to applicant i.e. employer, friend, etc.

1. _____

2. _____

3. _____

Barbara Jordan
United States Representative

"My faith in the Constitution is whole. It is complete. It is total." The powerful voice of Texas Congresswoman Barbara Jordan was hypnotic. Many Americans were watching her 15-minute speech on television and listening to it on the radio that day. Her voice was clear and strong. Barbara went on to say she could not sit by and watch the Constitution be destroyed. What could she be talking about?

In 1974 the people of the United States needed answers. The media reported that President Richard Nixon may have broken the law. Barbara was part of a special House Judiciary Committee who met and looked at the evidence against the President. They had to decide if he covered up the fact that some of his aides had broken the law. The group's answer was very important because if they decided that the evidence supported the accusation of the cover-up, they would recommend to the House of Representatives that President Nixon be impeached.

Barbara believed the Constitution to be a set of laws for all Americans guaranteeing them fair treatment, and its integrity must be maintained. She said no one was above the law—not even the President of the United States. When it was her time to speak, Barbara said that the President has certain duties and responsibilities outlined in the Constitution. Barbara said her group must use the facts in making their decision and set aside any personal biases they felt for the President. They must weigh the evidence carefully and do what was right.

In July of 1974, the group voted. They said that they had looked at the evidence, and they believed the President should be charged with breaking the law. Barbara said, "There were tears behind doors and off camera after the vote, from both men and women." Before the impeachment process could be continued in the full House of Representatives, President Richard M. Nixon resigned from office on August 8, 1974.

Barbara was very sad about the events that had led to the resignation of the President, but her faith in the Constitution and United States of America remained intact. "I would be the last person to claim that our nation is perfect. But we have a kind of perfection in us because our founding principle is universal—that we are all created equal regardless of race, religion, or national ancestry." Barbara had fought to preserve the Constitution and won.

Barbara Jordan died in January of 1996. She was 59 years old.

Bonuses for Barbara

In 1974 Barbara was selected for many honors: Democratic Woman of the Year by the Women's National Democratic Club; Woman of the Year in Politics by *Ladies Home Journal*; Woman of the Year by *Time* magazine; and Woman Who Could be President by *Redbook* magazine.

What do you remember from your reading?

Fill in the blanks of the following sentences with the correct word(s). Then locate the answer in the word search. You will have to look up, down, backwards, diagonally, and of course forward to find them.

```
C A R M D C U V J E R I N O
L T E L B A T R O F M O C T
E P S M P Y R A I C I D U J
G N I K A E P S R T X E S W
N E G O C I L A U Q E H L M
O S N V F A I T H S P C Q U
L F E I K D I G U W H A T S
D I D C I T A R C O M E D R
S C M W S J N E U T S P O X
U A Y N D B G S L E W M K E
V J O F I J E C O H T I C L
I C O N S T L F M T W O B A
```

1. Barbara said "My _____ in the Constitution is whole."

2. Barbara believed the _____ was for all people, not just a select few.

3. Barbara Jordan was affiliated with the _____ political party.

4. Barbara believed President Nixon had broken the law and should be _____.

5. Barbara Jordan was a congresswoman in the _____ of Representatives.

6. Barbara Jordan was famous for her _____ abilities.

7. President Nixon was not impeached, rather he _____ from office August 8, 1974.

8. Barbara was a member of the special House _____ Committee.

9. Although it wasn't easy to judge the President, Barbara was _____ with the committee's findings.

10. Barbara Jordan believed all people were _____ regardless of race, religion, or national ancestry.

11. On the back of this paper or a separate sheet, write a few sentences, in your own words, about Barbara Jordan. Use the following words in your sentences.
   a. media
   b. evidence
   c. accusation
   d. impeached
   e. biases

Research

The incident in history that lead to President Nixon's resignation is often called Watergate. Consult a research book to find answers to the following questions. Write a brief paper of at least two paragraphs telling of your findings.

Why was the incident called Watergate? Who were the principle players in the coverup? What happened? How were the people punished? What happened to President Nixon after he resigned? Who became the new President?

Write an Epitaph

An epitaph is a commemorative inscription usually put on a tombstone or a monument. The writer of an epitaph tries to capture the essence of the deceased as well as what others thought of the person. Major accomplishments are included as well the person's date of birth and date of death.

Write an epitaph for Barbara Jordan.

You are a writer who has been selected to write Barbara Jordan's epitaph which will be displayed on a plaque near her grave. Consider the following questions to help you organize your thoughts. For some of the questions, you will need to consult additional resources.

1. When was Barbara Jordan born? When did she die?

2. Where was Barbara born?

3. Where did she attend college? Which degrees did she earn?

4. What profession did she practice?

5. Was she ever elected to public office? If so, name the offices she held?

6. What are the distinguishable characteristics of Barbara?

7. Think of three major events in her life.

8. What did other people think of her?

9. Think of three adjectives or adjective phrases that describe her.

10. What special awards or honors did Barbara receive in her life? There are at least five.

_____

_____

_____

_____

_____

Using the information in your answers, write an epitaph for Barbara Jordan. It should be written in paragraph form.

_____

_____

_____

_____

One More Step

Once the class has finished the assignment, get into groups and read one another's epitaphs. Select the best ones from the group to read aloud to the class.

Coretta Scott King
Civil Rights Leader

Coretta Scott King walked through the doors of the newly completed Martin Luther King, Jr., Center for Nonviolent Social Change in Atlanta, Georgia. The beautiful complex contained Martin's tomb, the Chapel of All Faiths, the King Library and Archives, a museum, office space, a gift shop, a theater, and an auditorium. It had been a dream of hers since 1968 when she began planning the memorial for her husband, slain civil rights leader, Dr. Martin Luther King, Jr. For years she traveled around the country to raise the $10 million needed for the construction. She gave speeches and attended fund-raisers. She always spoke of her husband with much affection, reminding people of his work and for what he stood. She promised to continue the mission Martin began, and the King Center was a way to teach people of his work.

When an assassin's bullet cut short the life of her husband at age 39, Coretta became a single mother with four young children to raise. She was a dedicated mother with goals to fulfill her husband's dreams as well as a few of her own. Coretta threw herself into her work. She led protest marches and made hundreds of speeches. She helped produce several award-winning films about their life and work. She wrote a book entitled, *My Life with Martin Luther King, Jr.*, which was widely read.

Coretta worked with the International Peace Movement, and in 1985, she and two of her children were arrested in front of the South African Embassy in Washington, D.C. They were protesting the South African government's policy of racial segregation known as apartheid. Coretta has never hesitated to call high officials, senators, presidents, and representatives, to remind them to speak out on behalf of peace and equality for all races. "We have to dare to dream of genuine brotherhood and sisterhood between the races before we can bring it into being," she says.

In 1986 Coretta accomplished another goal she had set for herself after her husband's death in 1968. Martin's birthday, January 15, became a national holiday in the United States. It is a day set aside to honor Martin's work for peace and racial harmony.

Coretta Scott King has devoted her life to keeping her husband's dreams alive. Yet she has worked hard to fulfill her own dreams, too. "I never thought I could save the world, but I felt that I could work and make some contribution, to make things better for people who come after me."

Kings' Continuing Contribution

More than half a million visitors visit the Martin Luther King, Jr., Center for Nonviolent Social Change in Atlanta each year. Training classes are held at the Center which teach Martin's methods of solving problems nonviolently. People from all walks of life, from gang members to police officers, have attended these classes.

Name _____ Date _____

What do you remember from your reading?

Use the clues to complete the crossword puzzle.

DOWN

1. Dr. Martin Luther King, Jr., was a man of ___.
2. Members of the King family were arrested for protesting this
3. One of the words in the formal name of the center Coretta built in honor of her husband.

ACROSS

4. Coretta's husband was ___ when he was 39 years old.
5. Dr. King's birthday, is a ___ holiday.
6. Coretta wants ___ between the races.
7. Coretta had ___ of her own.

8. Choose a word from your reading to fit each meaning.

a. a monument by which we remember a person or event _____

b. a self-imposed duty _____

c. one who carries out a plot to kill a prominent person _____

d. a policy of social separation of races _____

e. an official policy of racial segregation in the Republic of South Africa _____

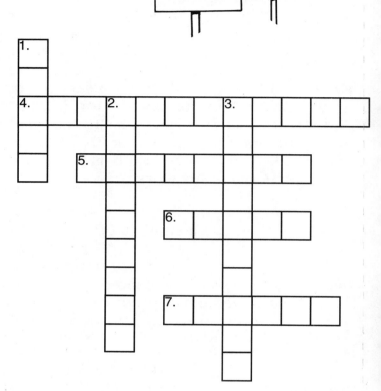

Research

People like Coretta Scott King and Dr. Martin Luther King, Jr., have played vital parts in the Civil Rights movement. There are other personalities who have made important contributions, too. Rosa Parks, The Little Rock 9, and Jesse Jackson are a few of them. Using the examples listed or one of your own, write a brief paragraph describing the person and his/her contributions. Be sure to include a topic sentence and supporting details.

Name _____ Date _____

Write a Business Letter

Your teacher has told you that you will be doing a report on the Martin Luther King, Jr., Center for Nonviolent Social Change, the memorial complex Coretta worked so hard to have built for her husband. You would like to send away to the Center for information.

Fill in the following requested information to have the correct form of a business letter. The body of the letter is where you will need to state your purpose for writing and specifically request the information on the Center. Include a thank you toward the end of the body.

The address for the Center is:

Martin Luther King, Jr., Center for Nonviolent Social Change
449 Auburn Avenue Northeast
Atlanta, GA 30312

_____

_____

_____
The **return address** is your address. Do not include your name.

_____
Today's date.

_____

_____

_____
The **inside address** is the address to which you are writing.

_____
The **salutation** is Dear Sir or Madam.

_____

_____

_____
The **body** is where you state your purpose and make your requests.

_____
The **close** is Sincerely, Yours truly, or something like this.

_____
The **signature** is your signature.

_____
Your name, printed.

One Step More

The address for the Center is correct. If you would like to receive information, rewrite your letter in the same format, and mail it.

Thurgood Marshall
Supreme Court Justice

Thurgood Marshall passed through the entrance of the United States Supreme Court at First and East Capital Streets, N.E., in Washington, D.C. Above the doorway, etched in stone, were the words, "Equal Justice Under the Law." He paused to read them and smiled. For so many years those words did not mean the same for white people and African Americans. There was no "Equal Justice" as far as African Americans were concerned. But today history would be made, he thought.

The Justices called on the confident African-American lawyer to present his case. For years he had planned and waited for a case like this. Other cases he had tried had prepared him well. He believed strongly in what he had to say. The name of this case was Brown versus the Board of Education of Topeka, Kansas, and it dealt with school segregation.

The year was 1954. White children and African-American children did not attend the same schools. This was the law. Thurgood did not think this was fair for the African-American children because often their schools were inferior. Their materials were old, their school buildings were run down, and their desks were not as good as those of the white children. Thurgood argued before the court that because of these discrepancies, segregated education was not equal education, and the law guaranteed equal education for all.

Thurgood was well-prepared and gave many examples. He cited psychological studies that said that African-American children felt inferior because of the inferior manner in which they were educated. He said that African-American children were placed at a disadvantage, and this was not fair to them—it was not what the law promised. The Supreme Court unanimously agreed. Thurgood won the case, so now children of all races could attend the same schools.

Unfortunately schools were not immediately integrated. The Court had said in its ruling that the states must integrate the schools "with all deliberate speed." Many states took a long time to start the process of integrating the classrooms, while others did absolutely nothing toward doing what the Court had ordered. Thurgood continued the fight for integration and filed case after case to force school districts to do what the Supreme Court had ruled. Meanwhile he worked on other cases to end discrimination in voting, housing, criminal procedure, and public places.

In 1967 President Johnson asked Thurgood Marshall to serve as a Supreme Court Justice. He became the first African American to hold a seat on this high court. It was an appropriate position for a man who had done so much in his life to guarantee "Equal Justice Under the Law."

Memorize, Mr. Marshall!

When Thurgood misbehaved in school, his principal sent him to a quiet place to memorize parts of the Constitution. He said that it did not keep him from getting into trouble, but it did help him later in life when he was arguing cases!

What do you remember from your reading?

Using what you have learned from your reading about Thurgood Marshall, answer the following questions in complete sentences.

1. Why did Thurgood think history would be made the day he argued Brown versus the Board of Education of Topeka, Kansas?

    _____

2. Why did Thurgood believe that segregated education was not equal under the

    law? _____

3. Winning the Brown versus the Board of Education of Topeka, Kansas, case was not an immediate end to separate schools for the races. Why?

    _____

4. What was significant about President Johnson's appointing Thurgood Marshall as a Supreme Court Justice?

    _____

5. Write each of the words in bold type in the following sentence and its meaning on the lines below.

Psychological studies **unanimously** found that the **discrepancies** caused by **inferior** schools and educational tools for African-American students was a form of **discrimination** that caused those students to feel less important.

a. _____

b. _____

c. _____

d. _____

e. _____

Research

Thurgood Marshall worked many years as an attorney for the NAACP. Consult research books to learn the history of this organization and its purpose. Write your findings in a short paper of at least two paragraphs. Be sure to include specific details. Don't forget to define the acronym, NAACP.

Dinstinguish Between Fact and Opinion

Judges like Thurgood Marshall often must listen to a case and decide what is true based on facts alone. Sometimes there are many other things that are said, but unless there is proof that the things took place, then they are considered opinion. A judge must only use *facts* in deciding a case.

Read the following passage very carefully. Afterward you will be asked to determine whether the sentences that follow are *fact* or *opinion* based on the story.

• Bryson Thomas raced home on his red Diamondback bicycle to watch a rerun of his favorite Star Trek episode. He was already five minutes late. Although he knew he was supposed to put his bike in the garage, he left it on the sidewalk in front of his house.

When the show was over, he went outside to get his bike, but it was gone. He looked around but didn't see it or anyone. So he went searching for his bike. He saw his friend Alex who lived two streets away on Split Oak Drive. Alex said he had seen a boy riding a red bike about 10 minutes before Bryson arrived. Bryson became very mad and said, "That boy stole my bike!" The two friends ran off to look for the boy on the red bike.

Three blocks away Alex and Bryson caught up with the boy on the red bike to discover the bike was a Schwinn. Sad and disappointed, Bryson returned home to hear his dad tell his mom that Bryson would have to be punished because he left his bike on the sidewalk again.

Read the following sentences carefully. If the sentence is a fact, write an F on the blank line. Remember that a fact is true and can be proven. If the sentence is an opinion, write an O on the blank line. An opinion is a belief or a conclusion without any proof.

____ 1. Bryson Thomas was not allowed to leave his bike on the sidewalk.

____ 2. Someone stole Bryson's bike.

____ 3. Alex said he saw the thief 10 minutes prior to Bryson's arrival.

____ 4. Bryson and Alex live in the same neighborhood.

____ 5. Bryson has a bad temper.

____ 6. Bryson's bike is a red Diamondback.

____ 7. As it turns out, the boy on the red bike was riding a Schwinn.

____ 8. Bryson was going to be punished for leaving his bike on the sidewalk.

____ 9. The Thomas family own a television.

____ 10. Bryson's father found Bryson's bike and put it away in the garage.

You are the detective.

Write a paragraph describing what you think really happened to Bryson's bike.

Colin Powell
War Hero/Military Adviser

In 1989 Colin Powell had a difficult decision to make, though after 35 years of military service, this was not a military decision. He could work for a publishing agent in New York, giving speeches and perhaps writing a book. He could make as much as $1 million a year! On the other hand, he had been asked to accept an appointment to the highest military position in the United States. He thought about the pros and cons of each position and discussed it with his family and friends. His decision made, Colin Powell became Chairman of the Joint Chiefs of Staff. He was 52 years old. This made him the youngest man ever to hold this position.

This was the crowning point for Colin Powell's distinguished career in the Army. During his years of service, Colin received many honors and medals for his brave actions. One of these was the Soldier's Medal, awarded after Colin risked his own life to rescue four people from a smoking helicopter wreck.

The helicopter had been carrying its five passengers over a section of Vietnam, a country in Asia. The pilot wanted to land the helicopter in a small area. As he brought the chopper close to the ground, one of the propellers hit a tree. Suddenly the helicopter crashed to the ground and began to burn. Major Colin Powell was one of the five passengers. He jumped from the helicopter safely, but he realized that the other three passengers and the pilot were still trapped inside. In spite of the smoke and danger, he returned to the helicopter four times to rescue them all. As he helped the last man out, the helicopter burst into flames.

Colin Powell's leadership as Chairman of the Joint Chiefs of Staff helped the United States achieve its decisive victory in the Persian Gulf during 1991's Operation Desert Storm. After the war Powell returned to his hometown and spoke to the students at his old high school, Morris High, in the South Bronx. His advice to them was, "Stick with it. Stay in high school and get the diploma. Don't think you are limited by your background. Challenges are there to be knocked down."

Colin Powell has fought bravely for his country in wars, lead troops in battles, advised presidents, and negotiated with other leaders to avoid conflicts. He even thought about running for president in 1996. He has been a great leader and an inspiration to all United States citizens.

Think About This!

Colin reported to Fort Bragg in North Carolina when he first joined the Army. North Carolina was not like New York. He couldn't even order a hamburger at a drive-in. African Americans had to go to the back door for their food. Colin saw segregated water fountains and rest rooms. Even the officers clubs were separate for white and African-American officers. These things made him angry.

Name _____ Date_____

What do you remember from your reading?

Using what you have learned from your reading about Colin Powell, answer the following questions in complete sentences.

1. What was special about Colin's appointment as Chairman of the Joint Chiefs of Staff? _____

2. What did Colin Powell do to merit winning the Soldier's Medal?

   _____

   _____

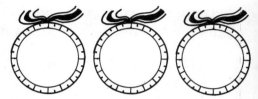

3. What was the advice Colin Powell gave to the students at his old high school?

   _____

   _____

4. What did Colin Powell do in 1996? _____

   _____

5. In your own words, write five sentences about Colin Powell using each of the following words:

a. military_____

b. publishing _____

c. decisive_____

d. negotiated _____

e. inspiration _____

Research

Colin Powell will be remembered for his part in Operation Desert Storm. Find out more about this war. You may ask family members as well as doing some reading. Write a page-long report about it. Use complete sentences in your writing.

Write About the Author

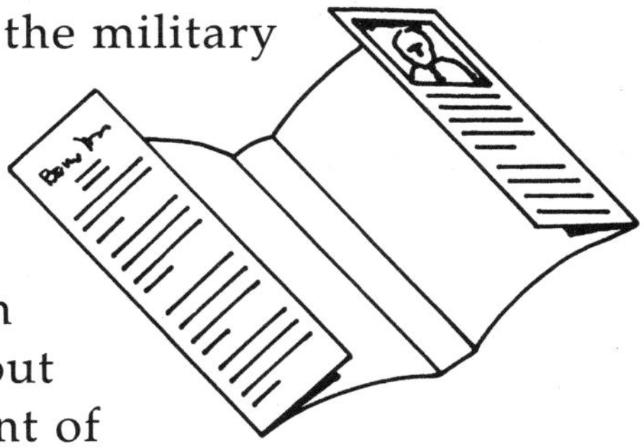

Colin Powell has written a book about his experiences in the military and politics. When someone writes a book, the publisher usually includes, on the inside of the back cover, some copy about the author.

Look at some books in your classroom or library to get an idea of the kind of information usually found in a book about the author. If you were to write the *About the Author* segment of a book written by Colin Powell, what would it say? Write your segment below.

_____

_____

_____

_____

_____

_____

_____

_____

Now you are the author!

Now imagine that you have written a book. What kind of information would the publisher include about you? Write an *About the Author* segment for your own book.

_____

_____

_____

_____

_____

_____

_____

_____

Name _____ Date _____

Unit 3 Review
Tom Bradley, Shirley Chisholm, Barbara Jordan, Coretta Scott King, Thurgood Marshall, Colin Powell

Write the answers to the following questions using complete sentences.

1. Why did Tom Bradley join the police force after he graduated from college? _____

   _____

2. What was Shirley's occupation when she was not involved in politics?

   _____

   _____

3. For what decision regarding President Nixon was Barbara Jordan's group responsible?

   _____

   _____

4. In what ways has Coretta Scott King carried on with the dreams of Martin Luther King, Jr.?

   _____

   _____

5. What was accomplished in the case of Brown vs. the Board of Education of Topeka, Kansas, the case for which Thurgood Marshall became best known?

   _____

6. For what act did Colin Powell receive the Soldier's Medal?

   _____

7. Write each of the words in bold type in the following sentence and its meaning on the lines below.

   The **distinguished** leader was an **inspiration** to all and showed **evidence** of strong **faith** when she did not let **discrimination** interfere with her **mission**.

   a. _____

   b. _____

   c _____

   d. _____

   e. _____

   f. _____

8. Write briefly about the way in which racial segregation or inequality affected the lives of all the people in this unit, and what they may have done to change the situation. Use the back of this paper or a separate sheet.

Guion Stewart Bluford, Jr.
Astronaut

Colonel Guion Stewart Bluford sat strapped in his seat aboard the space shuttle Challenger. A few minutes past 2:30 a.m. on August 30, 1983, the countdown began. "Ten, nine, eight..." Colonel Bluford listened as the seconds passed. "Three, two, one..." The 100-ton Challenger lifted off the launch pad and soared above the clouds, 180 miles above Earth, carrying the first African-American astronaut into space.

Colonel Bluford's preparation for this day had begun many years earlier. After joining the Air Force in 1964, he flew 144 combat missions in Vietnam. He was awarded more than two dozen medals and awards during his 3,000 hours of logged air time. Yet Guion wanted to do more.

When he returned from Vietnam, he earned his master's degree in aerospace engineering from the U.S. Air Force Institute of Technology. Soon he began testing and evaluating new airplanes and aircraft systems. In 1978 soon after he received his Ph.D. in aerospace engineering, Guion applied to the astronaut program with NASA (National Aeronautics and Space Administration). He was one of 35 people selected for the program from nearly 9,000 applicants.

He reported to Houston, Texas, at the Johnson Space Flight Center where he spent the next six months in intensive training. He had to learn to operate the space shuttle computers, instruments, and remote manipulator. He had to attend classes in medicine, astronomy, geology, and aerodynamics. The work was grueling.

When the Challenger lifted into space that August day, it began a six-day flight. There Guion's training was put into practice. He was responsible for launching a $45 million communications and weather satellite. He also participated in medical tests to discover why some astronauts experience motion sickness. Challenger and its crew landed on September 5, at Edwards Air Force Base in California.

Two years later on October 30, 1985, Colonel Bluford was again a crew member on a Challenger mission. This time the space shuttle with its astronauts orbited Earth 111 times during which 76 scientific experiments were performed.

Guion Stewart Bluford, Jr., has never been afraid of challenges. He sets goals for himself and works to accomplish them. "If you want to succeed, you must work hard, dedicate yourself, and make the necessary sacrifices...." he said. "Once you set goals for yourself, you should doggedly pursue them until you achieve them."

Space Race

In 1957 the Soviet Union launched Sputnik I, the first space satellite. Within a year the United States created NASA. In 1961 Yuri Gagarin, another Soviet citizen, became the first man to orbit Earth. Commander Alan B. Shepard of the United States was sent into space 23 days later.

Name _____ Date _____

What do you remember from your reading?

Using what you have learned from your reading about Colonel Guion Stewart Bluford, answer the following questions in complete sentences.

1. What was significant about the August 30, 1983, Challenger flight?

   _____

   _____

2. Approximately what percentage of the applicants were accepted in the space program the year Colonel Bluford applied?

   _____

3. On the initial flight, in what way did Colonel Bluford use the medical training he had received at NASA?

   _____

4. How many days did Colonel Bluford's first flight into space last?

   _____

5. Write a synonym for each of the following words.

   a. combat _____

   b. engineering _____

   c. intensive _____

   Write the meaning of each of the following words.

   d. manipulator _____

   e. aerospace _____

Space Survey

Space travel is a fascinating subject for many. The United States has been involved in numerous space missions—some successful, some not successful.

Take a survey. Ask your parents, relatives, and neighbors about specific space flights they can recall and discuss with you. Record the names, dates, and details they tell you. Try to create a time line of America's space travel with the details you have.

Before you begin your survey, be sure to have the questions you wish to ask the participants written down. You many want to organize a chart for recording your data.

Name _____ Date _____

The Space Shuttle's Orbit

Once the space shuttle is in orbit around Earth, it is guided by small rockets. No fuel is required to keep the shuttle moving because gravity, and the high speed at which it is moving, keep it in orbit. If the space shuttle were to stop moving, it would fall straight to Earth. If gravity ceased, but the space shuttle continued moving, the shuttle would continue going straight. Gravity pulls the shuttle toward Earth so the orbit is curved like Earth's curvature.

Simulate a space shuttle orbit.

To simulate a space shuttle in orbit, you will need three items: a plastic cover with a small outer ridge (whipped topping cover will do); a small, round, weighted object (something like a marble), and a pair of scissors.

The plastic cover will simulate the gravity that keeps the shuttle in orbit. Its center is Earth. The small weighted object will be the space ship.

1. Place the round object on the plastic cover and push it until it travels around the rim simulating the curved orbit of the shuttle. Remember gravity and speed keep it moving.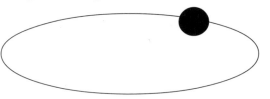

2. What would happen to your space shuttle (round object) if the gravity (plastic rim) were removed? _____

    _____

3. To find out, take your scissors and trim away a few inches of the plastic rim. Place the round object on the plastic cover again and push it around the edge. What happens? _____

4. Draw the path your round object took once the gravity was removed.

5. Why did your shuttle take this path? _____

Shuttle Super Facts

When it is time for the shuttle to return to Earth, it fires rockets in the direction the shuttle is headed. The result is that the shuttle's speed is decreased. Keep in mind that the gravity is the same so the shuttle is pulled closer and closer to Earth. It enters the atmosphere slowing even more until it glides to a landing. Small rockets help guide the ship.

Mae C. Jemison
Astronaut

In 1985 Mae Jemison had just returned from working with the Peace Corps in West Africa. She had accomplished many goals so far in her life, but there was one she had had since childhood that she needed to satisfy. She wanted to be an astronaut. Upon her return to the United States in 1985, she applied to the astronaut program at the National Aeronautics and Space Administration (NASA). On January 28, 1986, an unfortunate event took place in the space program. The Spaceship Challenger exploded shortly after launching killing all astronauts on board. NASA temporarily suspended its astronaut selection process. Sad but not deterred, Mae said, "… it was very sad because of the astronauts who were lost," but in no way was she going to give up wanting to be an astronaut.

As a child, Mae loved to read, and consumed books about science, science fiction, and astronomy. "I ended up being constantly aware of the world around me because of my own interest," she said. Mae grew up in the 1960s when people in the United States were excited about the space program and space travel. Nearly every little boy and girl had at one time said they wanted to become an astronaut. Yet for Mae the dream was more than a passing wish. She knew it would one day come true.

Mae graduated early from high school and because her grades were so good, she received a National Achievement Scholarship to Stanford University where she earned a degree in chemical engineering. In the fall of 1977, she entered Cornell University's medical school, and graduated in 1981. Mae joined the Peace Corps and, from January 1983 through July 1985, worked in Sierra Leone and Liberia in West Africa helping the needy people there.

With her on-going desire to be an astronaut, she reapplied for acceptance with NASA and was later notified that she was one of 15 candidates selected from a field of over 2,000. Mae joined the NASA program in 1987 and completed a one-year training program in August 1988 which qualified her as a mission specialist. In 1991 she was selected for the space flight on the Endeavor.

On September 12, 1992, the space shuttle Endeavor was ready on the launch pad at the Kennedy Space Center in Florida. Inside, the seven astronauts sat strapped into their seats ready for mission control to begin the countdown. One of the astronaut's childhood dream of becoming an astronaut had come true. Mae and the other astronauts waited as the seconds were counted down to liftoff. The Endeavor began to rise and it soon soared above the clouds—taking in it the first African-American woman into space.

Well-Rounded Mae

"Science is very important to me, but I also like to stress that you have to be well-rounded. One's love for science doesn't get rid of all the other areas. I truly feel someone interested in science is interested in understanding what's going on in the world. That means you have to find out about social science, art, and politics."

Famous African Americans 5-6, SV 6792-1

What do you remember from your reading?

Using what you have learned from your reading about Mae Jemison, answer the following questions in complete sentences.

1. What effect did the explosion of the Space Shuttle Challenger have on

   Mae?_____

   _____

2. How did Mae's love for reading create the foundation for her future?

   _____

   _____

3. Why did Mae have to reapply to the space program when she returned from West Africa?

   _____

   _____

4. Although science is important, why did Mae say one should know about other things as well?

   _____

5. Write a brief answer to each of the following questions.

   a. For what reason might a student be *suspended* from school?_____

   b. Name something that might be *consumed* at lunch. _____

   c. What is a *chemical* that you might find in your house? _____

   d. To what college would you like to gain *acceptance*? _____

   e. For what reason might you see a *specialist*? _____

Research

Mae went to West Africa to work with the Peace Corps. What do you know about the Peace Corps? You may need to consult a research book to find specific details such as when it was started and by whom. Who may join the Peace Corps? What do the participants receive in return for their service? Write your findings in complete sentences in a brief report of one-half page.

Name _____ Date_____

Test Weightlessness and Gravity

Astronauts do not feel their weight if there is no gravity pulling on them. The farther into space one goes, the less gravity he encounters. That's why astronauts float about in the space shuttle freely. There is no gravity to pull them down.

<u>Weightlessness</u>: Objects in the space shuttle are all falling at the same rate of speed toward Earth. There is nothing the astronauts can put their feet on, so they float freely in the space shuttle. This is what causes weightlessness. If you jump on a trampoline, you feel weightless when you are in the air. Astronauts feel this sensation the entire time they are in space.

Experiment with weightlessness.

You will need a Styrofoam cup, some water, and a sharp object to pierce a hole in the cup.

1. Hold the cup over a sink and fill it with water. Pierce a small hole on the side near the bottom of the cup. What happens?_____

2. Now suppose the cup were the space shuttle accelerating toward Earth. The cup and the water would be traveling the same speed. What do you think would happen?

    _____

3. Hold the filled cup high above the sink and drop it. What happens to the water flow from the hole? _____

    Why does this happen? _____

<u>Gravity</u>: Over 300 years ago an Italian scientist named Galileo found that gravity makes all things fall at the same speed no matter how heavy or light they are. Some people find it hard to believe that a lead ball weighing 10 pounds and a tennis ball weighing 6 ounces will fall at the same speed. Let's test Galileo's findings.

Experiment with gravity.

For this experiment you will need a friend, and 6 different items of various weights. Make a chart to write in the names of the items you will compare. Things like a sheet of paper will need to be crumpled in a ball so the surface area will not be restricted by airflow.

Stand at the top of some stairs or as high as you can get. Hold two different objects, one in each hand. Stretch out your arms, keeping your hands level, and drop the objects at the same time. Have your friend record the results of which item hit the ground first.

From your data, what can you say about Galileo's findings over 300 years ago?

Geraldine "Jerry" Pittman Woods
Medical Consultant and Civic Leader

"I remember walking into a physiology course and seeing all the white students working with various instruments, which I'd never seen before. I said to myself, 'So that's the name of the game,' and I got up early every morning and stayed late every night," recalls Geraldine "Jerry" Woods. The year was 1944 and she had just begun her Ph.D. program at Harvard University. She was a good student and very involved with her studies. Jerry was often the only African American in her classes, and she was puzzled by this. In the coming years she became instrumental in increasing minority participation in the sciences.

Jerry was born in 1921 in West Palm Beach, Florida. Her parents, although only educated through the eighth grade, placed great importance on education. They made careful investments early in their lives to make sure that their daughter could go to college without having to work herself. Jerry completed her studies without interruption, gaining a stellar reputation as an accomplished scientist. In 1945 she married, and soon afterward moved to California where she set up practice as a dentist.

In 1969 she was appointed by the federal government as special consultant to the National Institute of General Medical Sciences, National Institutes of Health (NIH). In this role, Jerry was able to address the issue that had so early in her life puzzled her, the lack of African Americans in the sciences. She was able to help develop two important programs at the NIH for minorities, the Minority Access to Research Careers Program (MARC) and the Minority Biomedical Support Program (MBS).

Go, Geraldine!

In 1975 she was elected as chair of the board of trustees of the school where she received her undergraduate degree, Howard University in Washington, D.C. In this position she became the first woman to head the board.

Since their implementation in the early 1970s, these programs have helped increase minority participation in the sciences. Through her research Jerry found that school counselors often discouraged minority students from entering the science and mathematics fields. The MARC and MBS were created to help minority schools be more competitive in applying for federal research monies and to encourage more minority students to seek fields of study in the areas of mathematics and science. In addition, MARC and MBS sponsor scholarships for professors at minority institutions. Students continue to benefit from the programs begun by Geraldine Pittman Woods in the 1970s. These students, who may not have chosen science careers had it not been for her efforts, are now engaged in study and research.

Name _____ Date _____

What do you remember from your reading?

Using what you have learned from your reading about Geraldine Pittman Woods, answer the following questions in complete sentences.

1. Geraldine was concerned about an issue involving her science studies.

   What was it? _____

   _____

2. Working with the NIH allowed Geraldine to help fellow African

   Americans. How? _____

   _____

   _____

3. What was one of the reasons Geraldine discovered that deterred minorities from entering science and math related fields?

   _____

   _____

4. Specifically how do students benefit from MARC and MBS?

   _____

   _____

5. Write a few sentences, in your own words, about Geraldine Pittman Woods. Use the following words in your sentences.

   a. physiology _____

   b. instrumental _____

   c. minority _____

   d. investments _____

   e. implementation _____

Research

Throughout her life Geraldine Pittman Woods has worked to better the educational opportunities of minorities. In February 1965 she was invited by the President's wife, Lady Bird Johnson, to the White House to launch a new educational program called Project Head Start. The program continues today and helps thousands of children gain a head start on their education.

What do you know about Head Start? Perhaps you, family members, or friends have attended a Head Start Program. Consult resource materials to find more information about this program. Write your findings in a two-paragraph report. Be sure to include specific details explaining the program, who started it, and when.

Determine the Amount of Blood in Your Body

Health care professionals spend a great deal of time studying blood. Every living person has blood in his or her body as it is necessary to sustain life.

Find out how much blood you have in your body.

For approximately every 32 pounds of weight, a person has about one quart of blood in his or her body. A person who weighs 160 pounds has about 5 quarts, and a child who weighs 80 pounds has about 2 1/2 quarts.

To determine the amount of blood in your body, fill in the following answers.

1. How much do you weigh? _____

2. Divide your weight by 32. _____

3. How many quarts of blood do you have in your

   body? _____

4. A person weighing 200 pounds has approximately how much blood in his or her body?

   _____

5. A person weighing 64 pounds has approximately how much blood in his or her body?

   _____

Pumping for More Information!

There are four types of blood. What are they? 1. _____   2. _____   3. _____   4. _____

Do you know your blood type? ___   How could you find out?_____

Name_____   Date_____

Unit 4 Review
Guion Bluford, Mae Jemison, Geraldine Pittman Woods

Write the answers to the following questions using complete sentences.

1. What was unusual about Colonel Guion Bluford's ascent into space?

_____

2. What event prevented Mae Jemison from entering the NASA space program in

   1986? _____

3. What did Geraldine Pittman Woods find in her research into the reasons for the
   lack of African Americans in the sciences?

_____

4. In what ways can other people, white and African-American, benefit from the
   achievements of the people studied in this unit?

_____

5. Use the clues to complete
   the crossword puzzle.

ACROSS:

1. Geraldine Pittman Woods was
   instrumental in increasing whose
   participation in the sciences?

2. What type of mission did Colonel
   Bluford fly in Vietnam?

3. Mae Jemison's degree was in what
   type of engineering?

DOWN:

4. Guion Bluford's Ph.D. was in what
   type of engineering?

5. A word to describe the training
   that astronauts must undergo.

Famous African Americans 5-6, SV 6792-1

Dominique Dawes
Olympic Gymnast

The young gymnast, standing just over five feet tall, balanced on the edge of history. No one else in the last 25 years had done what she was poised to do. It was the 1994 United States National Championships, and Dominique Dawes was about to clinch her fourth medal in the individual competitions. Her strongest event was yet to come. In the floor exercise she perfectly executed her "signature move of a combination of somersaults, whip backs and handsprings up one diagonal and back again in the opposite direction," and it was just too much for the other gymnasts to match. Dominique Dawes, known as Awesome Dawesome to her gym mates, was awarded her fourth individual gold medal and along with it a place in history.

Gymnastics have been a large part of Dominique's life. "I was about six when my parents put me in because I had a lot of energy," she explained. Her mom, Loretta, said Dominique could slide down the stairs of her family's home on her stomach, then perform cartwheels across the living room and out the front door. Loretta Dawes wanted to channel her daughter's energy in a positive area, so she enrolled her in coach Kelli Hill's gym which met at a nearby shopping mall. Dominique loved gymnastics and was soon begging to sleep in her leotard. Her strong and muscular body made her a natural at gymnastics, and by the time she was 12, she was winning medals at national competitions. Her desire to succeed at the sport was evident. Coach Hill said, "Whatever I wanted Dom to do, she would do it."

But Dominique's parents didn't push her into her sport. Instead, it was her responsibility to get up and get ready for her 6:00 a.m. practices before school. When she was ready, she had to wake her mom to take her to the gym. Dominique eventually worked up to training about 36 hours a week. "You just get used to it after a while. I finish at 8:10 every night, eat dinner, and go to sleep." Her parents reminded her often, "If you don't like your sport, quit. Don't do it to make Mom or Dad happy."

Dominique was always driven. Coach Hill explained, "I've had several children who were as God-given talented, but the burning desire that Dom has wasn't there." That desire, along with determination and dedication to the sport, have earned Dominique top medals in national and world gymnastic competitions including a gold team medal and a bronze individual medal in the 1996 Summer Olympics in Atlanta, Georgia. Dominique says, "Ten years down the road, I think I'll know that this was all worthwhile. It was worth working the amount of hours I've put into it. Everything is paying off."

Dominique's Dedication

When most gymnasts join the rank of the elite, they change coaches, choosing more high-profile, well-known ones with sometimes bigger and better gyms. Not Dominique! She has remained loyal to her first coach, Kelli Hill, who taught her how to execute her first proper somersault when she was only 6 years old.

73

What do you remember from your reading?

Using what you have learned from your reading about Dominique Dawes, answer the following questions in complete sentences.

1. How did Dominique Dawes secure her place in history at the 1994 United States National Championships?

    _____

    _____

2. What early evidence did Dominique's parents have of her gymnastic abilities?

    _____

    _____

3. Why didn't Dominique's parents push her into gymnastics?

    _____

    _____

4. To what does Coach Hill attribute Dominique's success?

    _____

5. Write a sentence, in your own words, using each of the following words.

    a. poised _____

    b. executed _____

    c. channel _____

    d. evident _____

    e. elite_____

Research

Dominique Dawes was winning national competitions in gymnastics when she was 12 years old. Perhaps you or some of your classmates are involved in a sport or activity for which you have won medals, special titles, or awards for your participation. Examples could be dance, baseball, hockey, in-line skating, modeling, motorcross, agriculture, or a religious activity.

Find 10 classmates who excel at a certain activity. Write the person's name and the awards she or he has won. Design a chart to display your findings. Try to find a variety of activities, as well as an equal number of males and females.

Name _____   Date _____

Work With Graphs

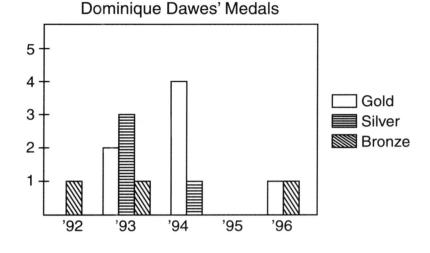

Study the following bar graph carefully to answer the questions below.

Write the correct answers on the lines provided.

1. In which year did Dominique win the most gold medals?

    _____

2. How many total medals did she win in 1993? _____

3. In which year did she not win a medal? _____

Now it is your turn to design a pie chart.

You are going to design a pie chart using the information from the bar graph above. The pie chart is drawn for you so you will need to determine the appropriate amount of space to represent her medal winnings. Answer the following questions to help you know how to divide the pie chart.

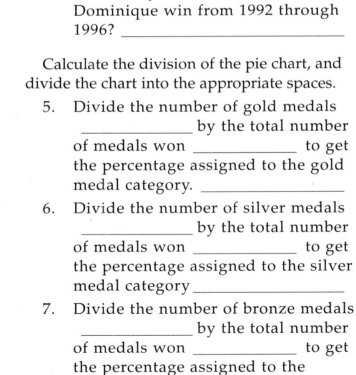

1. How many medals were gold?

    _____

2. How many medals were silver?

    _____

3. How many medals were bronze? __

    _____

4. How many total medals did Dominique win from 1992 through 1996? _____

Calculate the division of the pie chart, and divide the chart into the appropriate spaces.

5. Divide the number of gold medals _____ by the total number of medals won _____ to get the percentage assigned to the gold medal category. _____

6. Divide the number of silver medals _____ by the total number of medals won _____ to get the percentage assigned to the silver medal category_____

7. Divide the number of bronze medals _____ by the total number of medals won _____ to get the percentage assigned to the bronze medal category_____

    Famous African Americans 5-6, SV 6792-1

Gail Devers
Olympic Runner

In 1992 the Olympic Games were in Barcelona, Spain. Gail Devers stood ready on the track, one of the eight fastest women in the world. Soon the 100-meter race would begin.

Four years earlier Gail was well on her way to another Olympics, in Seoul, Korea. She had been training hard and was ready to run the 100-meter hurdles. Bobby Kersee, Gail's coach since 1984 when she entered college, had made her believe in herself. Gail was a winner, and Bobby knew it.

What happened next was a mystery. Gail began to feel strange. Her running times were slowing down, and she did not qualify for the Olympic games in Seoul. Then she began to suffer migraine headaches, loss of sleep, fainting spells, injuries to her muscles, and shaking she could not control. She experienced loss of vision in her left eye. For two years her doctors tried treatments for many different illnesses, but none of them were the right one. Meanwhile, Gail's health continued to decline. Finally one doctor found she had a rare illness called Graves' Disease. Gail was frightened by this news, but at least now she knew what was wrong with her. Unfortunately, when Gail began her treatment, she became even sicker. The radiation was destroying the tissue in her body, especially her feet. At this point it had become extremely painful for Gail to even walk, and some of the doctors thought they should operate to remove her feet.

Instead, the doctor who had correctly diagnosed Gail decided to change her treatment, and she began to improve quickly. Just one month later, as soon as she could walk, Bobby convinced her to get on the track again. Gail thought he must be kidding—she couldn't even put her shoes on her sore feet yet. But she did go to the track, at first carefully stepping around the loop in her stocking feet. Before long she was able to put on her track shoes and to begin running again. She began to train for the Olympics in Barcelona.

In Barcelona the starting gun fired, and the race began. Eight women sprinted from the starting blocks. Just a year-and-a-half after thinking she might never walk again, Gail Devers flew across the finish line in first place. She had won the gold for the 100-meter dash.

Gail competed once again in the 1996 Olympics in Atlanta, Georgia, and again she won gold in the 100-meter dash. But Gail says her illness is something she will never forget. "I'm a stronger person," she says, "I've said before that there's nothing that can come up in my life that I can't get over after going through what I did...It taught me so much."

Go, Gail!

Gail's high school in National City, California, had no track team and no coach. Gail practiced alone and was the only runner representing her school at track meets. "It was the loneliest feeling in the world," says Gail. Still she won many races.

Gail still takes medicine for Graves' Disease. She watches what she eats and gets plenty of rest.

Famous African Americans 5-6, SV 6792-1

Name _____ Date _____

What do you remember from your reading?

 Using what you have learned about Gail Devers from your reading, answer the questions below using complete sentences.

1. In how many Olympic games has Gail Devers competed? In what years were

    they held? _____

2. What were the differences between Gail's track experiences in high school and

    her experiences in college? _____

3. How many gold medals has Gail won for the 100-meter dash?

    _____

4. What is the name of Gail's illness? How did her illness affect her performance?
   How does it affect her life now?

    _____

    _____

5. Choose a word from your reading that has the same meaning as the word(s) in
   bold type.

    a. The climbers had many **obstacles** to overcome. _____

    b. You have to have a lot of talent to **have what is required** for this group.

    _____

    c. I hope his condition does not **get worse**. _____

    d. Gail Devers was given **a special kind of therapy** to help her recover from

    Graves' Disease. _____

    e. As soon as we have **found out the nature of** the problem, we can solve it.

    _____

Research

Research Graves' Disease. Before you begin, identify three or four questions you
will want answered when you do your research. Write a report, at least a half-page
long, about the disease.

Write a Script

Become a playwrite. Write the script for a skit about Gail Devers using what you know about her from your reading and using your imagination to create dialogue.

Who are your principle actors? (You may choose classmates.)

Gail Devers_____

Bobby Kersee_____

Doctor #1 _____

Doctor #2 _____

Doctor #3 _____

Other _____

What kind of simple costumes can the actors wear so that the audience will easily recognize the part they are playing?

Gail Devers_____

Bobby Kersee_____

Doctors _____

Other _____

What kind of props will the actors need, if any?

Gail Devers_____

Bobby Kersee_____

Doctors _____

Other _____

Now write a script with simple dialogue for your skit. Try to give each actor at least five lines. Remember, you are writing dialogue for your script; but you are also writing instructions for the actors telling them when to be on stage, where to be on stage, and when each scene begins and ends.

One step more

Get some actors together, practice, and perform the play for your classmates. Some tips to remember while you are practicing:

Speak clearly and loudly enough for the whole audience to hear you.
Stand facing the audience whenever possible.
Have fun!

David Robinson
Scholar/Athlete

In 1984 a young man named David Robinson was graduating from high school in Florida. He had been a star player on his high school basketball team, and college scouts had been watching. Many colleges wanted David to come and play basketball for them. But David had decided that he wanted to follow his father's footsteps and join the Navy. His high scores on the entrance exams enabled him to attend the United States Naval Academy at Annopolis, Maryland. At the Academy David would be trained to become an officer in the United States Navy.

David was a very bright student—at the age of 14 he was taking computer courses at local colleges. His parents sent him to a special school so that he could reach his learning potential. Surprisingly basketball was not easy for David. About the sport at which he also excelled, David said, "The game didn't come naturally to me. Basketball was more work than fun."

Although David continued to play basketball at Annapolis, he concentrated on his studies of computer science. He also continued to grow. David grew six more inches in college to a height of 7'1"! And the basketball world had not forgotten about David. They had watched him play and grow at Annapolis, and the professional teams now wanted him. The NBA selected David first in the 1987 draft. But David had made a commitment to the Navy. Though by now he really did want to play basketball, he also wanted to do the right thing and keep his promise. He would stay at the school for the full five-year term.

But sometimes life has a way of working things out for us. Because of David's height the officials at Annapolis knew that he would not be able to work on the Navy's submarines or ships, nor would he be able to fly the Navy's planes. They allowed David to leave Annapolis early, shortening his service from five years to two.

David had many teams to choose from. He elected to go with the San Antonio Spurs. Basketball fans had been waiting years to see David play. They were not disappointed. David was chosen as the best new player in the league in 1987. David scored 23 points in his first game with the Spurs against the Los Angeles Lakers. Said basketball great Magic Johnson, "Some rookies are never really rookies. Robinson's one of them." David continues to be a star basketball player. A Spurs teammate said, "David's got so much talent it's ridiculous!"

Two more points!

David Robinson quit his high school basketball team when he was 14. He was afraid he would be dropped from the team! He didn't play for the school again until he was a senior.

David's father taught him how to read music and to play the piano!

Name_____ Date_____

What do you remember from your reading?

Using what you have learned about David Robinson from your reading, answer the questions below using complete sentences.

1. Why did David choose to attend a naval academy? What was it called?

   _____

2. What did David say about his ability to play basketball? _____

   _____

3. What happened to David in college that excited the basketball scouts?

   _____

4. What was the effect of David's growth on his career as a naval officer?

   _____

5. Choose the correct word to fill in each blank.

basketball player	professional potential	scouts courses	submarines Navy	rookies commitment

a. Many _____ went to see David Robinson play college basketball.

b. The scouts could see that David had the _____ to be a great player.

c. The scouts wanted David to play _____ basketball.

d. David had made a five-year _____ to the Navy.

e. David was the best of the _____ in 1987.

Research

Find out more information about the U.S. Naval Academy in Annapolis, Maryland. How old is it? Who was its founder? What are the entrance requirements? Write a report with your findings. Include some of the Academy's history and some information about what the students' lives are like. Your report should be one page long. Remember to use complete sentences.

Learn About Airplanes

If David Robinson had not grown too large to fit in the Navy's jets, he may have become a pilot! Airplanes are certainly a familiar sight to all of us, but how much do you know about them?

1. Find a book about airplanes, or look in an encyclopedia.

2. Draw a picture of any kind of airplane or jet.

3. Label the following parts, if applicable:

    wings

    fuselage (body)

    tail assembly

    landing gear

    engine

4. Label other parts that are characteristic of the kind of plane or jet you have drawn. Not all planes will have the same equipment.

5. Write a half-page report telling about the plane you have drawn. Was it one of the first planes? Is it one of the most modern? Did or does it have a specialized purpose? Is this type of plane still used today?

_____

_____

_____

_____

_____

6. List some of the uses of airplanes. Write a sentence describing each use.

_____

_____

_____

_____

Emmitt Smith
Professional Football Player

The graduate began his walk across the stage to receive his college diploma and shake the university president's hand. John Lombardi, the University of Florida's president, extended his hand as the graduate's name and degree were read for all to hear, "Emmitt Smith, Bachelor of Science, Public Recreation."

In May of 1996, Emmitt Smith fulfilled a promise he made to his mother, Mary, six years before when he skipped his senior year in college to play professional football for the Dallas Cowboys. "I told her I was coming out of school to begin my NFL career. I also told her that I would be back at the University of Florida every off-season until my degree was finished. I was serious about that commitment," explained Emmitt. Earning his bachelor of science degree made Emmitt the first in his family to receive a college degree.

Emmitt proved that, although it delayed his graduation, his choice to begin his professional football career before he finished college had been the right choice. From the time he left Gainesville, Florida, as the Dallas Cowboys' first-round draft choice, until the day he graduated, he had amassed fortune and fame as a professional football player and businessman.

During those six years Emmitt earned four NFL rushing titles, and he led the Dallas Cowboys to win three Super Bowl titles. In May of 1996, Emmitt was paid $3.4 million a year to play for the Cowboys, and he received several more million dollars in endorsement income. Moreover he owned three very successful companies. Emmitt is a driven man. "There's so much more I need to accomplish," he says. "I have so much room to grow, both as a player and as a person. If you're satisfied, you're finished. You can never be satisfied."

Mary Smith, Emmitt's mother, said she is glad he completed his college education. "I'm so proud of Emmitt. It's rare to see someone in his profession do this." Emmitt was proud of his accomplishment, too. "I always felt a little hypocritical talking to kids when I hadn't accomplished my academic goals myself. Now I won't be lying."

Emmitt's Endeavor

Emmitt says, "I'm chasing after legends, after Walter Payton and Tony Dorsett and Jim Brown, and Eric Dickerson, after guys who made history. When my career's over, I want to have the new kids, the new backs say, 'Boy, we have to chase a legend to be the best.' And they'll mean Emmitt Smith."

Famous African Americans 5-6, SV 6792-1

Name _____ Date _____

What do you remember from your reading?

Use the clues to see which words you need to find in the word search. Look up, down, backwards, diagonally, and of course forward to find the words.

1. Emmitt's degree was in Public ____.

2. The president of the University of Florida when Emmitt attended

3. The team for which Emmitt Smith was a first round draft choice

4. Where in Florida is the University from which Emmitt graduated?

5. Emmitt believes one should never be ____.

6. Emmitt says he wants to one day be considered ____.

7. Emmitt was the first in his family to be a college ____.

8. The number of years Emmitt played professional football before he completed his college degree

9. Emmitt is a successful football player and ____.

10. For what does Emmitt hold many NFL titles?

11. Using the words below and a separate sheet of paper, write a brief paragraph, in your own words, about Emmitt Smith.

   a. recreation
   b. draft
   c. amassed
   d. endorsement
   e. hypocritical

```
N A M S S E N I S U B S O R
O R N Y A F O N T M L F U D
W U N O T U M G A C O D L E
H O S B I R U S H I N G R L
T D O W S T C A L E X E H L
E B F O F N A S G S P T A I
I R J C I M G E L R V A P V
E X I S E I L U R K S U P S
T I M A D O C N B C A D Y E
H H K L O J C K I S E A E N
R S A L U C L O M B A R D I
S E Y A T T I M M E O G I A
T U S D I M L E Q U I R T G
```

Research

Emmitt receives endorsement income as well as income from three companies he owns. Utilize your library's resources (Internet if you have it) to discover which products Emmitt endorses and what kind of companies he owns. Report your findings in a report of two paragraphs. Be sure to include a topic sentence and supporting details.

Write a Radio Spot

Often a sports celebrity's name and face are synonymous with a certain product. Perhaps a company may even name a product after a celebrity. Emmitt Smith has received millions of dollars from endorsing certain items in print media, television, and radio spots.

When a company wishes to advertise on television and radio, it must pay a great deal of money for a small amount of air time. The costs of broadcast media ads are determined by the time of day the ad will run and during which segment or show it will run. Advertisers must be very precise in their ad, as they want to say the most they can in this small amount of air time.

You are an advertisement writer.

Your job is to write a radio spot (ad) for a new product that has just hit the market. You may choose the item. It can be a new kind of athletic shoe, a new car, a new kind of clothing, a new CD, a new kind of food, or anything else you think you can legally sell. You will need to introduce your audience to the new product, tell about its features, cost, where it can be bought and anything else you may wish to include. But you only have 20 seconds to do it—the average length of a radio advertisement.

On the lines below write the words to your 20-second radio spot advertising your new product. If you plan to use specific music, include instructions on how it will be played and when. Celebrity voices must be labeled, too.

Read the words of your ad enough times so that it will take exactly 20 seconds.

_____

_____

_____

_____

_____

One More Step

Call your local radio and television stations' advertising departments to find the average cost of broadcast air time. Compare time of day, and length of ad for television and radio. Make a chart of your findings.

When is the most expensive time to advertise on radio? _____

On television? _____

Frank Thomas
Baseball Star

It was the bottom of the tenth inning and the score was still tied. The Chicago White Sox and the New York Yankees were battling for the 1993 American League Western Division lead. The White Sox badly needed the win. The Yankees had failed to score at the top of the tenth, and now the Sox had their turn at bat. Steve Farr, a tough pitcher, stood on the mound ready to hurl the next pitch. To the plate came the Sox's 25-year-old first baseman, Frank Thomas. Frank stood 6 feet, 5 inches tall, and he weighed nearly 260 pounds. He dug his feet in and glared at Steve who was in his windup. The ball was just what Frank had been waiting for. The crack of the bat was heard over the roaring crowd. The ball continued climbing as it passed over the center fielder's head and into the seats of the upper deck. Frank Thomas, also known as "The Big Hurt," had done it again. He clinched another win for the Sox with his powerful batting.

Tenacious Thomas!

As a freshman in high school, Frank went out for baseball, but was cut from the team. Frank was not discouraged, however. The experience only made him work harder.

Frank Edward Thomas was born in Columbus, Georgia, on May 27, 1968. By the time he entered high school he had begun showing athletic promise. But he had to work hard at being a good athlete; it didn't come naturally to him. By his junior year, Frank was a standout in basketball, football, and baseball. He wanted to be a professional athlete, he just didn't know which sport. Auburn University in Alabama offered Frank a football scholarship to play as a Tiger tight end. Before he accepted he wanted to make sure he could play baseball, too, if given the chance.

Frank didn't see much action on the football field that first year, so he decided to try out for the baseball team. After one day of practice, Coach Hal Baird knew Frank was not an average walk-on, "He was one of those rare athletes that, the very first time we saw him on our field, we realized he was something special." Soon, Frank had positioned himself as the starting first baseman and by far the best hitter on the team. His coach called him the greatest walk-on player in Southeastern Conference (SEC) history. His powerful hitting made him a standout with batting averages well over .350. Coach Baird's praise was genuine, "...I'd say he's the best hitter I've ever coached. People just stop what they're doing to watch Frank take batting practice."

Frank's batting and offensive skills landed him a spot on the major league White Sox in August of 1990. He had a .318 batting average, 32 home runs, 109 RBIs, and he crossed the plate 104 times that first year. This was enough to earn him his nickname, "The Big Hurt." He was named to the Associated Press and *Sporting News* All-Star teams. Indeed his first year proved to be a glimpse of things to come. By the end of 1994, he was a 26-year-old with four years in the majors and a string of credits to his name. He had established himself as one of the greatest hitters in the history of baseball. One of his teammates, Julio Franco, said, "Playing with Frank is like being part of history."

What do you remember from your reading?

Using what you have learned about Frank Thomas from your reading, answer the following questions in complete sentences.

1. Why did Frank accept the football scholarship to Auburn University?

    _____

    _____

2. What do you think made Frank decide to try out for Auburn's baseball team?

    _____

    _____

3. How did his college coach describe Frank?

    _____

    _____

4. What kind of rookie year did Frank have?

    _____

    _____

5. Write an antonym for each of the following words:

    a. standout _____

    b. genuine _____

    c. offensive _____

    d. credits _____

    e. discouraged _____

Research

Frank Thomas had a little sister named Pamela who died of leukemia when she was two-and-a-half years old. Frank was very close to her and says of her death, "You never get over something like that." In her honor Frank charges a certain amount of money for an autograph and sends the money to a special organization. He also donates the money from the sale of his Gold Leaf baseball cards to this organization.

How much does Frank charge for an autograph? _____

To which organization does he send the money? _____

Name _____ Date _____

Read a Chart
Batting Averages of Frank Thomas 1986 - 1994

Team Affiliation	Year	Batting Average	Home Runs	RBIs
Columbus High School	1986	.450	13	52
Auburn Tigers	1987	.359	21	68
Auburn Tigers	1988	.385	9	54
Auburn Tigers	1989	.403	19	83
AA Birmingham Barons through August,	1990	.323	18	71
Chicago White Sox August - December,	1990	.330	7	31
Chicago White Sox	1991	.318	32	109
Chicago White Sox	1992	.323	24	11
Chicago White Sox	1993	.317	41	128
Chicago White Sox	1994	.353	38	101

Study the chart of Frank Thomas's batting averages to find the answers to the following questions. Write your answers on the lines provided.

1. For what team did Frank play when he had the best batting average?

   _____

2. In which year did he have the most RBIs? _____

3. How many home runs did Frank hit the last half of 1990? _____

4. If you added the home runs Frank hit his first year in college with the first full year in the majors, how many would you have? _____

5. In which year with the Auburn Tigers did Frank have the most RBIs?_____

6. In which major league year did Frank have the best batting average? _____

7. How many home runs did Frank hit his last year in high school? _____

8. How many home runs did Frank hit in college? _____

9. For whom was Frank playing when he had his poorest batting average?

   _____

Eldrick "Tiger" Woods
Golf Professional

Sports fans watched and wondered if this young golf phenomenon could do what no one had ever done. It was a hot August day in Oregon, and Eldrick "Tiger" Woods stood on the edge of history. Two years before he became the first African American to win the men's U.S. Amateur golf title. He won it a second time in 1995. No one had ever won three straight amateur titles, but could Tiger change history?

He had been playing all week, easily disposing of five other opponents. Now he faced his last test, golfer Steve Scott. Steve had won his first five matches that week, too. The two golfers were the last players left. One would win, and one would lose.

Steve jumped out to a big lead early in the match. Tiger remained calm and slowly fought back. By the end of the day, he had come back to tie Steve, who later said, "Against Tiger Woods, no lead is safe." With the match even, the two golfers had to go into sudden death where the first golfer to sink a hole wins the tournament. They tied the first extra hole. On the second hole, Tiger needed only to make a one-foot putt to win. When the golf ball landed in the bottom of the cup, the young man from Cypress, California, had made history again. Tiger Woods had won his third U.S. Amateur golf title in a row, and he was only 20 years old!

Tiger turned pro August 28, 1996, and shortly thereafter signed over $60 million in endorsement deals, and a $2.2 million book deal—that's not counting the money he gets when he wins a tournament. "He's not playing for the money," Davis Love III, another golf opponent, said. "He's trying to win. He thinks about winning and nothing else."

History continues to be made or at least recreated by this young phenomenon. The face of golf has changed because of Tiger Woods. People who have never watched golf are suddenly interested in seeing him play. The seven-week tour after he turned pro brought out an extra 150,000 fans. Peter Jacobsen, an opponent of Tiger's, said, "He's the greatest player in the the history of the game." Maintenance workers, presidents of companies, senior citizens, and lots of young people join the crowds. "To look out there and see so many kids, I think that's wonderful. They see someone they can relate to, me being so young... It's really nice seeing more minorities in the gallery," he says. Tiger loves what he is doing and it shows. He smiles and looks like he's having a good time. As Tiger plays his rounds, he throws balls to youngsters. "I remember when I was a kid, I always wanted to be a part of it. I always wanted to be connected somehow." Today, Tiger Woods is definitely connected!

Tiger's Triumphs

1st to win three U.S. Junior Amateur golf titles

1st to win both the Junior Amateur and the U.S. Amateur titles

---

1st African American to win a U.S. Amateur title

1st to win three U.S. Amateur titles in a row

Name _____ Date _____

What do you remember from your reading?

Using what you have learned in your reading about Tiger Woods, answer the following questions in complete sentences.

1. Who was Tiger's opponent in the sudden death of the U.S. Amateur in 1996?

    _____

2. How did Tiger make history in 1996? _____

    _____

3. How has Tiger changed the face of golf? _____

    _____

4. How do we know Tiger enjoys what he is doing? _____

    _____

5. Write each of the words in bold type and its meaning below the following sentence.

    Tiger Woods proved himself to be a young golf **phenomenon** by **disposing** of Steve Scott, yet another **opponent**, at the U.S. **Amateur** golf **tournament** in 1996.

    a. _____   _____

    b. _____   _____

    c. _____   _____

    d. _____   _____

    e. _____   _____

Research

Tiger Woods has signed for over $60 million in endorsements. Which companies will be paying Tiger this money, and what products do they have? The number of lines do not necessarily represent the number of companies.

Company _____ Products _____

Company _____ Products _____

Company _____ Products _____

Name _____ Date _____

Write a Friendly Letter

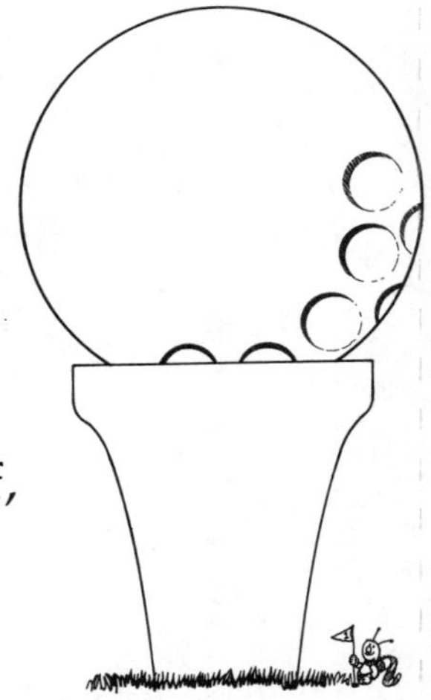

Some say Tiger Woods is a man who began changing the face of golf before he was 20 years old! He loves the sport and the fans who come to see him play. He especially enjoys the young people because he remembers when he was younger and wanted so much to be connected to the sport and to those who played it.

You are going to write a friendly letter to Tiger. In the body of the letter, you may tell him how he has helped change your view of golf, you may congratulate him on his success, and you may ask him a question or two.

Supply the requested information to create the correct form of a friendly letter. Include your thoughts in complete sentences with appropriate punctuation.

_____

_____

_____

your address (don't include your name)

_____ today's date

Dear _____ ,

_____

_____

_____

_____

_____

_____

_____

_____

_____

Sincerely,

_____

your name

Unit 5 Review
Dominique Dawes, Gail Devers, David Robinson, Emmitt Smith,
Frank Thomas, Tiger Woods

Write the answers to the following questions using complete sentences.

1. What were Dominique Dawes' responsibilities with regard to her practices?

   _____

2. How does Graves' Disease affect Gail Devers' life today?

   _____

3. Why did David Robinson feel that he should stay at the U.S. Naval Academy rather than joining a professional basketball team in 1987?

   _____

4. Which of Emmitt Smith's accomplishments was the one of which his mother was most proud? _____

5. What happened when Frank Thomas went out for baseball his freshman year in high school?

   _____

6. How has Tiger Woods changed the way people think about the sport of golf?

   _____

   _____

7. Write a brief answer to each of the following questions.

   a. If you **executed** a perfect cartwheel in your living room, what might be the result?

   _____

   b. What might you need to achieve in order to **qualify** for a college academic scholarship? _____

   c. What is something you might be doing if college **scouts** were watching you? _____

   d. What is your favorite form of **recreation**? _____

   e. What is something that could cause an athlete to become **discouraged**? _____

   f. What should you do to an **opponent** after a game or match? _____

8. Write a few sentences describing what the athletes in this unit have in common.

   _____

   _____

Famous African Americans Gr. 5/6
Vocabulary List

academic	decline	inauguration	porter
acceptance	degradations	inferior	potential
accusation	diagnosed	insight	prejudice
adolescent	discouraged	inspiration	priority
adorned	discrepancies	instrumental	private
aerospace	discrimination	intensive	professional
amassed	disposing	interpret	psychological
amateur	distinguished	intolerance	public
ambition	doctorate	intrigue	publishing
ancestors	domestic	investments	pursue
apartheid	draft	lyrics	qualify
applause	dyslexia	manipulator	radiation
assassin	editor	media	reaction
associate (n.)	elite	medic	reassurance
biases	encouragement	melody	recreation
cadence	endangered	memorial	refuge
campaign	endeavor	military	rookies
captivating	endorsement	minority	safari
channel	engineering	mission	scholarship
characters	evidence	modest	scouts
chemical	evident	negotiated	segregation
collateral	executed	nomination	sharecroppers
combat	faith	offensive	specialist
commitment	freelance	opponent	spousal
consequences	genuine	oppression	standout
consultant	humor	ovation	suspended
consumed	hurdles	perseverance	tournament
controversial	hypnotic	persistent	transatlantic
conventional	hypocritical	persuaded	unanimously
credits	identify	phenomenon	unity
critique	identities	physiology	venture
culture	impeached	pinnacle	
decisive	implementation	poised	

ANSWER KEY – Famous African Americans 5/6

P.7 Assessment Test 1. They are all writers. 2. laugh 3. politics 4. astronauts 5. athletes 6. He is a famous publisher; i.e. *Ebony* and *Jet*. 7. Whitney Houston sings "pop," and Leontyne Price sings opera. 8. Answers will vary. 9. medicine. 10. At the 1996 Olympics during a social event. 11. Barbara Jordan 12. Tiger Woods 13. Gordon Parks 14. Thurgood Marshall 15. Babyface 16. through 20. Answers will vary.

P.10 1. She wanted the people to get along peacefully. 2. She was able to be herself and live in a stable environment. It was fun at Momma's, having the store as the nucleus of activity in the community. 3. She believed that when she last spoke (at the trial), she caused the death of a man. 4. *I Know Why the Caged Bird Sings* 6. a. hypnotic b. cadence c. unity d. inauguration e. insight RESEARCH: Answers will vary.

P.11 Answers will vary.

P.13 1. He sat naked in the "middle passage" of a slave ship for several days, researched information in the National Archives, and went on a safari to his native land. 2. They were the basis for his book, *Roots*. 3. It created the desire to write his own stories. 4. He started getting his stories published. 5. a. transatlantic b. ancestors c. freelancer d. safari e. degradation RESEARCH: Answers will vary.

P.14 Answers will vary.

P.16 1. He said he had decided once and for all to make it or die. 2. She moved the family to Chicago so he could go to high school. 3. It had never been done. 4. The reasons for John's success were hard work, perseverance, and dedication. 5. Answers will vary. RESEARCH: Answers will vary.

P.17 Answers will vary.

P.19 1. It spoke to her about how African-American children feel about themselves. "If only I could have blue eyes like white children..." 2. It was written in the language of African Americans without the author explaining the nuances. 3. She felt her life would be so much better if she had blue eyes like the white children. 4. She has won the Nobel Prize in Literature. 5. Answers will vary. RESEARCH: Answers will vary. There are six areas in which to win a Nobel Prize—chemistry, economics, physics, medicine, literature, and peace.

P.20 Answers may vary. 1. You can't judge something by its appearance. 2. Don't count on events before they happen. 3. Let's leave. 4. Don't judge someone until you have had his or her experiences. 5. People who speak up get results. 6. Once you have chosen a course, stick with it.

P.22 1. He had to buy a coat, get some lunch, and go to a movie. 2. The theater did not allow African Americans into their establishment. 3. Gordon's home was full of love but very poor. 4. Gordon's first movie was called *The Learning Tree*, and it was about his childhood. 5. Answers will vary. Examples: a. response b. persecution c. narrow mindedness d. motivation e. attempt RESEARCH: Answers will vary. Examples of Parks' books: *Shannon, Born Black, A Poet & His Camera,*

P.23 Answers will vary.

P.24 Unit I Review: 1. Maya Angelou wanted to write in a way that African-American readers would understand, and she did not want to worry about whether anyone else understood it or not. 2. Alex Haley experienced the voyage his ancestors took on slave ships, did extensive research, and traveled on safari to the village of his ancestors in Africa. 3. John Johnson put up his mother's furniture as collateral, borrowed $500, and got credit from printers to begin his first magazine, *Negro Digest*. 4. Toni had a conversation when she was a child with another little girl, who felt that if God would give her blue eyes, she would have a better life. 5. Gordon Parks was not allowed to try on a suit, eat dinner in a restaurant, nor to enter a movie theater. 6. Answers will vary. 7. Answers will vary.

P.26 1. He played a song from the soundtrack, and she liked it so much that she decided to sing it. 2. It was his first R&B Number One as a solo act. 3. He has had 16 Number One songs. 4. He thinks Prince, Stevie Wonder, and the Beatles are great songwriters. 5. He feels that although he has had some hits, he is in the process of growing. 6. a. melody b. lyrics c. associate d. interpret e. modest RESEARCH: *The Day*

P.27 Answers will vary.

P.29 1. It lasted for eight years. 2. Bill has been a bartender, a medic, an actor, a writer, a comedian, and a salesman. 3. Bill's humor is kind and gentle and relates to all people. 4. He returned to school to complete his degrees. 5. a. medic b. conventional c. doctorate d. humor e. identify RESEARCH: Answers will vary.

P.30 Answers will vary.

P.32 DOWN: 1. Caryn 2. casual 3. *The Color Purple* 4. theater 5. because ACROSS: 6. *Ghost* 7. dyslexia 8. eight 9. Whoopi Goldberg 10. bricklayer 11. laugh 12. Answers will vary. RESEARCH: Answers will vary.

P.33 Answers will vary.

P.35 1. She was nervous that she might not be a good actress. 2. The many people who went to see the movie and the success of its music. 3. Since she was a child, Whitney has known that music was in her soul. 4. Whitney says that they can get on each other's nerves, but that having a close family is what really matters. 5. Answers will vary. RESEARCH: Answers will vary.

P.36 Answers will vary.

P.38 1. It was the longest ovation in the history of the opera house. 2. Her college teachers convinced her to become a singer. 3. She did not have enough money to pay for the rest of the costs of going to school. 4. Leontyne became the first African American to appear in a televised opera. 5. Answers will vary. RESEARCH: Answers will vary. Examples of other operas Leontyne has performed are: *Aida, Porgy and Bess, Antony & Cleopatra, The Girl of the Golden West.*

P.39 Answers will vary.

P.41 1. It gave her her first public speaking opportunities. 2. It was a way she could escape her unhappiness. 3. He provided an environment with strict rules and high expectations. Oprah needed guidelines. 4. The call that asked her to be host on a morning talk show in Chicago changed her life. 5. Answers will vary. Examples are: a. decorated b. top c. shelter d. bookish e. youth RESEARCH: Answers will vary.

P.42 Answers will vary.

P.43 Unit 2 Review: 1. Babyface has a soft, gentle style and a way of bringing out the best in the singers with whom he works. 2. Bill Cosby was working at a club, and one night the owner asked him to stand in for the regular entertainment when they did not show. He was a great success. 3. Whoopi Goldberg has dyslexia, a disorder that makes it difficult for her to read. 4. Whitney Houston had never tried acting, and she was nervous that she would fail. 5. Leontyne Price was accepted into the school, but she did not have enough money to go. 6. Oprah says she would not trade places with anyone. She would do her job for free if she had to. 7. Answers will vary. 8. Answers will vary.

P.45 1. He received an athletic scholarship. 2. They gave him the gift of faith. 3. He was a member of the Los Angeles City Council in 1963. 4. He was African American and only 15% of the voters were African American; also, there had never been an African-American mayor in L.A. 5. a. sharecroppers b. priority c. public d. porter e. faith RESEARCH: Answers will vary.

P.46 Answers will vary.

P.48 1. Shirley devoted eighteen years of her life to politics. 2. Shirley wanted to make a difference for her people by helping them get better jobs, better places to live, and better schools. 3. Shirley made sure she got appointments to the right committees. 4. She was the first African-American woman to have a seat in the United States Congress, and she was the first African-American woman to run for the US presidency. 5. Answers will vary. RESEARCH: Answers will vary.

P.49 Answers will vary.

P.51 WORD SEARCH ANSWERS

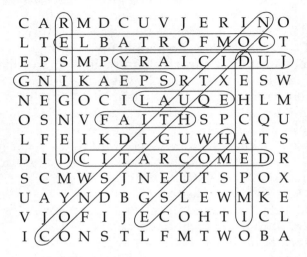

11. Answers will vary. RESEARCH: Answers will vary.

P.52 Answers will vary.

P.54 DOWN: 1. peace 2. apartheid 3. nonviolent ACROSS: 4. assassinated 5. national 6. unity 7. dreams 8. a. memorial b. mission c. assassin d. segregation e. apartheid RESEARCH: Answers will vary.

P.55 Answers will vary.

P.57 1. He felt he would win, and the decision would end segregation in schools. 2. The African-American children had inferior schools, books, and materials. 3. States took their time to integrate; some chose not to at all. 4. Thurgood was the first African American to sit on the court. 5. a. psychological; of or relating to the mind or emotions b. unanimously; in complete harmony or accord c. discrepancies; disagreement between facts d. inferior; situated under or beneath e. discrimination; a prejudiced act RESEARCH: Answers will vary.

P.58 1. F 2. O 3. O 4. F 5. O 6. F 7. F 8. F 9. F 10. O

P.60 1. He was the youngest man ever to hold the position. 2. He risked his life to pull four people from a burning helicopter. 3. He told them to stay in school and get their diplomas, not to be limited by their backgrounds, and to knock down challenges. 4. He considered running for the office of President of the United States. 5. Answers will vary. RESEARCH: Answers will vary.

P.61 Answers will vary.

P.62 Unit 3 Review: 1. He knew he needed a way to support himself while he was in law school. He also wanted to serve his city. 2. Shirley spent most of her life in the field of education. She was a director at a private nursery school and a child care center, and then educational consultant for New York City's Bureau of Child Welfare. 3. They had to decide whether or not President Nixon was aware of the fact that some of his aides had broken the law, and whether he covered up this information. 4. Corretta King built the King Center, gave speeches and attended fund-raisers, protested racial segregation in South Africa, and worked to make Martin Luther King, Jr.'s, birthday a national holiday. 5. The Supreme Court ordered that children of all races could attend the same schools. 6. Colin Powell rescued four people from a smoking helicopter before it burst into flames. 7. a. distinguished; eminent or recognized b. inspiration; the quality of exalting or inspiring c. evidence; the data on which a conclusion or judgment may be based d. faith; confident belief in the truth, value, or trustworthiness of a person, idea, or thing e. discrimination; acting on the basis or prejudice f. mission; a self-imposed duty 8. Answers will vary.

P.64 1. It carried the first African-American astronaut into space. 2. Approximately .38% (35/9000) of the applicants were accepted into the space program the year Colonel Bluford applied. 3. He participated in a medical test to discover why some astronauts experience motion sickness. 4. It lasted six days. 5. Answers will vary. Examples are: a. action, battle, engagement b. finessing, achieving, making c. complete, exhaustive, concentrated d. something controlled or operated by skilled use of the hands e. of or relating to the science or technology of flight SPACE SURVEY: Answers will vary.

P.65 2. The "shuttle" would fly out of orbit, away from the center. 3. The "shuttle" flies off the rim. 5. There was no gravity to hold the "shuttle" in place, but it still had its speed, so it flew off into space.

P.67 1. It made her sad, but it did not stop her from wanting to be an astronaut. 2. She read all the science, science fiction, and astronomy books she could put her hands on, thus increasing her knowledge and love for science. 3. Shortly before she went to West Africa, NASA had stopped appointing new astronauts because of the Challenger explosion. Upon her return, NASA was accepting new applicants. 4. It makes a person more well-rounded. 6. Answers will vary. RESEARCH: Answers will vary.

P.68 Answers will vary.

P.70 1. There were very few African Americans in her classes. 2. She was able to help develop two programs, the MARC and MBS, from which minority science students directly benefited. 3. Guidance counselors often discouraged minorities from entering these fields. 4. These programs help minority schools be more competitive in applying for federal grants and encourage minority students to seek math and science related studies. Also these programs help with scholarships for professors at minority schools. 5. Answers will vary. RESEARCH: Answers will vary.

P.71 Answers will vary.

P.72 Unit 4 Review 1. He was the first African-American astronaut. 2. The space shuttle, Challenger, exploded, killing all the astronauts on board. NASA temporarily suspended its astronaut selection process. 3. She found that school counselors often discouraged African-American students from entering the science and mathematics fields. 4. Crossword: ACROSS: 1. minority 2. combat 3. chemical; DOWN: 4. aerospace 5. intensive. Question #6. Answers will vary.

P.74 1. She won gold medals in all four of the individual events. 2. She had a lot of energy and could slide down the stairs on her stomach, do cartwheels across the living room and out the front door. 3. They wanted it to be her choice alone. 4. In addition to her talent, Dominique is very driven. 5. Answers will vary. RESEARCH: Answers will vary.

P.75 1. 1994 2. 6 total: 2 gold, 3 silver, 1 bronze 3. 1995 YOUR TURN: 1. 7 gold 2. 4 silver 3. 3 bronze 4. 14 total 5. 7/14 = 50% 6. 4/14 = 28.6% 7. 3/14 = 21.4%

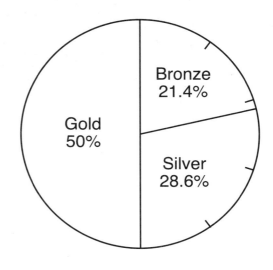

Famous African Americans 5-6, SV 0000-0

P.77 1. Gail has competed in two Olympic games; in 1992 and 1996. 2. Gail had no track coach in high school, nor did she have any team mates. 3. Gail has won the gold twice for the 100-meter dash. 4. Gail has Graves' Disease. The illness caused headaches, fatigue, fainting, muscle injuries, and shaking, all of which made Gail unable to compete. Now Gail has to take medication, watch her diet, and get plenty of rest to avoid complications. 5. a. hurdles b. qualify c. decline d. radiation e. diagnosed RESEARCH: Answers will vary.

P.78 Answers will vary.

P.80 1. David wanted to following his father's footsteps. He went to the U.S. Naval Academy in Annapolis, Maryland. 2. David said that basketball did not come easily to him. He had to work at it. 3. David grew to a height of 7'1" in college.
4. David was too tall for the Navy's planes and ships, so he was released from his obligation of five years of service. 5. a. scouts b. potential c. professional d. commitment e. rookies RESEARCH: Answers will vary.

P.81 Answers will vary.

P.83 WORD SEARCH ANSWERS

```
N A M S S E N I S U B S O R
O R N Y A F O N T M L F U D
W U N O T U M G A C O D L E
H O S B I R U S H I N G R L
T D O W S T C A L E X E H L
E B F O F N A S G S P T A I
I R J C I M G E L R V A P V
E X I S E I L U R K S U P S
T I M A D O C N B C A D Y E
H H K L O J C K I S E A E N
R S A L U C L O M B A R D I
S E Y A T T I M M E O G I A
T U S D I M L E Q U I R T G
```

11. Answers will vary. RESEARCH: Answers will vary.

P.84 Answers will vary.

P.86 1. He would be allowed to play baseball there if he wanted to. 2. He wasn't seeing much action on the football field. 3. He said he was a rare athlete and the greatest walk-on player in the history of the Southeastern Conference. 4. He had a great one—.318 batting average, 32 home runs, 109 RBIs, scored 104 times, and was named to the Associated Press and *Sporting News* All-Star team. 5. Answers will vary. Examples:
a. unobtrusive b. fake c. defensive d. debits e. encouraged RESEARCH: Answers will vary.

P.87 1. Columbus H.S. 2. 1993 3. 7 home runs 4. 53 home runs 5. 1989 6. 1994—.353 7. 52 home runs 8. 49 home runs 9. Sox—.317

P.89 1. It was Steve Scott. 2. He became the first to win three straight U.S. Amateur titles. 3. People who have never watched golf are suddenly interested, and more people are coming out to watch. 4. He smiles and seems to have a good time on the course. He talks to the people, especially the kids. 5. a. phenomenon; one outstanding for a quality or achievement b. disposing; dealing with conclusively c. opponent; one who opposes another in a contest d. amateur; an athlete who has never participated in a sport for money e. tournament; a contest with a series of eliminations RESEARCH: Answers will vary.

P.90 Answers will vary.

P.91 Unit 5 Review 1. She was responsible for getting herself up and ready and waking her parents for a ride to practice. 2. Gail still has to take medicine, get plenty of rest, and watch what she eats. 3. David felt that he should honor his five-year commitment to the Academy. 4. Emmitt returned to the University of Florida to finish his studies and get his degree even after he had gained fortune and fame as a football player. 5. Frank was cut from the team. 6. More people from every different walk of life are becoming interested in the sport because of Tiger's personality and because he has shown that African Americans can compete and win in golf. 7. Answers will vary. 8. Answers will vary.